MARITIME HISTORY SERIES

Series Editor

John B. Hattendorf, *Naval War College*

Volumes Published in this Series

Pietro Martire d'Anghiera, et al.
The history of travayle in the West and East Indies (1577)
Introduction by Thomas R. Adams,
John Carter Brown Library

Alvise Cà da Mosto
Questa e una opera necessaria a tutti li naviga[n]ti (1490)
bound with:
Pietro Martire d'Anghiera
Libretto de tutta la navigatione de Re de Spagna (1504)
Introduction by Felipe Fernández-Armesto,
Oxford University

Martín Cortés
The arte of navigation (1561)
Introduction by D. W. Waters,
National Maritime Museum, Greenwich

John Davis
The seamans secrets (1633)
Introduction by A. N. Ryan, University of Liverpool

Francisco Faleiro
Tratado del esphera y del arte del marear (1535)
Introduction by Onesimo Almeida, Brown University

Gemma, Frisius
De principiis astronomiae & cosmographiae (1553)
Introduction by C. A. Davids, University of Leiden

Tobias Gentleman
Englands way to win wealth, and to employ ships and marriners (1614)
bound with:
Robert Kayll
The trades increase (1615)
and
Dudley Digges
The defence of trade (1615)
and
Edward Sharpe
Britaines busse (1615)
Introduction by John B. Hattendorf, Naval War College

Pedro de Medina
L'art de naviguer (1554)
Introduction by Carla Rahn Phillips, University of Minnesota

Jean Taisnier
A very necessarie and profitable booke concerning navigation (1585?)
Introduction by Uwe Schnall,
Deutsches Schiffahrtsmuseum, Bremerhaven

Lodovico de Varthema
Die ritterlich un[d] lobwirdig Rayss (1515)
Introduction by George Winius, University of Leiden

Gerrit de Veer
The true and perfect description of three voyages (1609)
Introduction by Stuart M. Frank, Kendall Whaling Museum

The seamans secrets

(1633)

John Davis

A Facsimile Reproduction
With an Introduction by

A. N. RYAN, M.A., F.R.Hist.S.

Published for the
JOHN CARTER BROWN LIBRARY
by
SCHOLARS' FACSIMILES & REPRINTS
DELMAR, NEW YORK
1992

SCHOLARS' FACSIMILES & REPRINTS
ISSN 0161-7729
SERIES ESTABLISHED 1936
VOLUME 475

Printed and made in the United States of America

The publication of this work was assisted by a grant from the National Endowment for the Humanities, an agency of the Federal government

Reproduced from a copy in, and with the permission of, the John Carter Brown Library at Brown University

Library of Congress Cataloging-in-Publication Data

Davis, John, 1550?-1605.
The seamans secrets (1633) / John Davis ;
a facsimile reproduction with an introduction by A. N. Ryan
p. cm. —
(Scholars' Facsimiles & Reprints, ISSN 0161-7729 ; v. 475)
(Maritime history series)
Reprint. Originally published: London : Iohn Davvson, 1633.
Includes bibliographical references.
ISBN 0-8201-1475-8
1. Navigation—Early works to 1800.
I. John Carter Brown Library. II. Title.
III. Series: Maritime history series (Delmar, N.Y.)
VK551.D25 1992
623.89—dc20 92-21729
CIP

Introduction

John Davis of Sandridge, so called to distinguish between him and the contemporary seaman, John Davis of Limehouse, was born about 1550 at Sandridge, a few miles up river from Dartmouth in the county of Devon.[1] We can say of his early life only that by the later 1570s his proficiency as a seaman and navigator was such as to have led him into professional association with the Devonian gentleman adventurers, Sir Humphrey and Adrian Gilbert, who were promoters of English colonization in North America and of a renewed search for a passage around North America from the Atlantic to the Pacific: the Northwest Passage, which Martin Frobisher had failed to find in three voyages of 1576-78.[2]

The association with the Gilberts brought Davis into contact with their half-brother, Walter Ralegh, an ardent advocate of colonial and maritime expansion, and with the famous mathematician and cosmographer, Dr. John Dee, an ardent advocate of the conquest of the Northwest Passage. Firm evidence of active planning dates from 1583 when Adrian Gilbert obtained a patent to seek a passage by way of the Arctic Seas to China and the Moluccas on behalf of himself and 'certaine Honourable personages and worthy Gentlemen of the Court and Countrey, with divers worshipfull Marchants of London and the West Countrey', of whom William Sanderson of London was said to be 'the greatest adventurer with his purse'.[3] At a political level the enterprise enjoyed the interest and influential backing of Elizabeth I's principal secretary, Sir Francis Walsingham.

In June 1585 Davis sailed from Dartmouth as 'Captaine and chief Pilot of this exployt' on the first of three memorable voyages which were to put his name on the map of the world. The main achievements of the first voyage were the exploration of the west coast of Greenland as far as the modern Godthåb, the crossing from east to west of what is now called Davis Strait to a point on Baffin Island just within the Arctic Circle, and the observation of Cumberland Sound. He cleared up some, if not all, of Frobisher's geographical misconceptions, established more clearly the relationship between Greenland and North America, and provided grounds for a renewal of hope in the existence of the passage.

In Davis's own mind there was little or no doubt. In 1586, on a voyage largely dedicated to extending the work of 1585, he battled his way up the Greenland coast to a latitude of 63°N. , crossed again to Baffin Island, and continued with a general survey of the American coast on his way southward. The high point of the 1587 voyage was to reach 72°; 12'N on the Greenland coast, which he named Hope Sanderson. He then made over to the American coast, explored fully Cumberland Sound, rediscovered Frobisher Bay, and returned home convinced, as he told Sanderson in a letter from Sandridge of 16 September, that, having found the sea open and forty leagues between land and land, 'the passage is most probable, the execution easie, as at my comming you shall fully know'.[4] Davis never put his optimistic theory to the test. Declining financial support, already apparent in 1587, the Armada campaign of 1588, and the death of Walsingham in 1590 terminated the enterprise. The search was not renewed until the early seventeenth century.

In 1595 Davis published *The Worlde's Hydrographical Description,* a work dedicated to the Lords of the Privy Council.[5] It was a declaration of faith in the existence of a navigable Northwest Passage and an account, perhaps even an *apologia*, of his own part as leader of the search. The arguments in support of the concept of the passage were modelled to some extent upon those elaborated by Sir Humphrey Gilbert in a treatise which was written about 1566 and published in 1576, the year of Frobisher's first voyage, as *A Discourse of a Discoverie for a New Passage to Cataia.*[6] Davis reinforced the academic arguments of Sir Humphrey and himself by reference to his own observations and practical experience gained during 1585-87. He also referred to the construction of a globe, the work of Emery Molyneux of Lambeth, which was largely financed, it would seem, by Sanderson.[7] The globe, the first to be constructed in England, illustrated Davis's discoveries. It was important to Davis not only for its delineation of the passage but also for its contribution to scientific navigation, especially in the northern regions, 'where the Meridians doe so speedily gather themselves together'.[8]

Davis finished with a statement of the benefits which would accrue to England 'by this passage being discovered'. He was compelled, however, by the demise of the syndicate which had financed the voyages of 1585-87 to look for opportunities elsewhere. To this end, he teamed up in 1591 with Thomas Cavendish. Cavendish, a landed adventurer from Suffolk, had become during 1586-88 the second English circumnavigator and had enriched himself by taking the Spanish galleon *Santa Ana*, bound from Manila to Acapulco, off Cape San Lucas, California, in November 1587. His aims in 1591 were the plunder of Spanish ships in the Pacific and the establishment of direct trade with China or Japan via the Strait of Magellan. He was anxious to acquire the services of Davis as a navigator and chartmaker with particular regard to the hazardous passage of the strait. Davis, who contributed to the fleet a vessel jointly owned by himself and Adrian Gilbert, had a different object from those of Cavendish. The arrangement between them was that Davis should part company off the Californian coast 'to search that Northwest discovery upon the backe partes of America'.[9] In other words he was to discover the Pacific terminus of the Northwest Passage which Drake had failed to find in 1579 on his voyage of circumnavigation.[10]

The last voyage of Cavendish (he died at sea) was a disastrous failure. Flawed by the leader's inadequacies as an organizer, it sailed under threat of logistical collapse. He neglected at a critical time, before attempting the strait, to appoint a rendezvous in the event of the fleet being dispersed; he entered, it would seem, into a state of depression, when deserted by the good fortune which he had enjoyed in 1586-88. Personal shortcomings by no means tell the whole story. Adverse winds and foul weather frustrated the efforts of both Davis and Cavendish to pass from the Atlantic to the Pacific. Davis displayed heroic fortitude and resolution in attempting to do so independently; but he was driven back and defeated. On return to England, he wrote that 'I have seene and tested the frowardnesse of the place [the Strait of Magellan], with the great unlikelyhoode of any passage to be that way'.[11]

Davis's career as an Arctic explorer was now over, but there was no lack of employment for him as navigator on voyages around the Cape of Good Hope to those Eastern Seas which he had hitherto sought in vain. The first of such services was as pilot to a Dutch East India Company based at Middleberg in the province of Zeeland, an appointment which testifies to his international reputation. In 1600 he was engaged by the newly-founded English East India Company as pilot major on the company's first voyage led by James Lancaster. He was recruited for service in 1604, the year after his return from the Lancaster voyage, by Sir Edward Michelbourne, a courtier who had been granted a licence, outside the East India Company's monopoly, by James I. This was to be his last service. Davis was killed by Japanese pirates in 1605.[12]

John Davis was both a product and a creator of the English native school of oceanic navigation which, as we can tell from his writings, he believed was foremost in the world. It had not always been so. At the time of his birth, the vast majority of English seamen were like the 'simple Fisher-man of Barking', described by William Bourne in *A Regiment for the Sea* as knowing 'Barking Creeke better than the best Nauvigator or Master in this lande'. But, continued Bourne, such were simple men who, if 'they should come out of the *Ocean* sea to seeke our chanel to come unto ye river of Thames, I am of opinion that a number of them, doth but grope as a blinde man doth, & if that they doe hit wel, that is but by chaunce, and not by any cunning that is in him'.[13]

As mid-century approached, mercantile entrepreneurs, statesmen ambitious for the increase of English wealth, and scholars were conscious of an enormous gap between the capacity of Spanish and Portuguese seamen to find and exploit new opportunities in the far distant oceans and that of contemporary English seamen to do the same. England did not lack skillful seamen, potentially capable of competing successfully with those of Iberia. Their skills were limited, however, by the backwardness of their nautical education. They had been reared in a very practical tradition that the secret of accurate navigation was the acquisition of knowledge of the depth of the sea, the nature of its bottom, of currents, tides, the lie of the land, the prevailing winds, and even the flight of birds, supported by the use of the compass, the log-line, the hour-glass, and the traverse board. These skills, which remained basic and essential, should not be despised. They had enabled English seamen to fish in Icelandic waters in the fifteenth century and, by exploiting increasing familiarity with the North Atlantic wind systems, to reveal to the world the great Newfoundland fishery. But they could not of themselves supply answers to the navigational problems which arose in the vast spaces of the oceans where many of the traditional techniques of pilotage were an insufficient guide to action, where remoteness from land put a premium upon the ability to calculate by astronomical observation and mathematical reasoning the accumulated distance and bearing from the last certain landfall after a lapse of days or even weeks.

When the work of education, prompted by an alliance of seamen and scholars, began in the late 1540s, the English were dependent upon foreign text books. The translation thereof was largely the work of Richard Eden who made his debut in 1553 with *A Treatyse of the Newe India* from the Latin of Sebastian Münster. There followed in 1555 *The Decades of the Newe Worlde or West India* from the Latin of Peter Martyr and in 1561 *The Arts of Navigation*, from the Spanish of *Brevo Compendio de la Sphera y de la Arte de Navegar* (1551) by Martín Cortés.[14]

The English were already liberating themselves from dependence upon foreign texts. A name to be remembered is that of Robert Recorde, writer of the first textbook of arithmetic in English. He went on to publish *The Castle of Knowledge* (1556), a treatise for the navigators of the Muscovy Company, and *The Whetstone of Witte* (1557), an elementary mathematical work which was dedicated to the Governors of the Muscovy Company. Author of the first English manual of navigation, *A Regiment for the Sea* (1574), was William Bourne of Gravesend. Bourne, whose professions were those of innkeeper, gunner, and surveyor, was a self-educated man dedicated to the instruction of 'simple' men whose social origins and opportunities for education were as humble and as limited as his own. The work ran into many editions, including some that were unauthorized, and was translated into Dutch. But the key work was Henry Billingsley's *The Elements of Geometrie of the most Ancient Philosopher Euclide of Megara* (1570), the first English edition of the works of Euclid. This was of immense influence in stimulating the study in England of mathematics, navigation, and hydrography, especially as the publication included a long and learned preface by John Dee in which he stressed 'how Mathematicall, the Arte of Navigation is'.[15]

A man much in tune with the new learning was Sir Thomas Gresham, financier and founder of the Royal Exchange. It was hardly a coincidence that, five years after the publication of *Euclid,* he made provision in his will for the foundation, following the deaths of himself and his wife, of a college whose curriculum would include applied mathematics and science. It was stipulated in the will that lectures were to be given in English to audiences of 'merchants and other citizens' and be tuned to their 'pitch and capacity'.

Gresham College opened its doors in 1598, two years after the death of Lady Gresham. By responding to a call for practical instruction in mathematics and nautical science on a formal basis, it offered an alternative to higher education in the universities of Oxford and Cambridge and helped to stimulate dedication to scientific advance and the multiplication of useful inventions. It was inspired by a growing consciousness that England's future wealth and greatness would be founded upon the seas. The educational program of Gresham College had been anticipated by John Dee when he accepted an engagement from the Muscovy Company to instruct its navigators; by his brilliant pupil Stephen Borough who pressed throughout his career for the diffusion of such instruction; by the scientist Thomas Harriot[16] who entered Ralegh's service with responsibility, among other things, for the advancement of navigation; by Richard Eden, Robert Recorde, William Bourne, and Henry Billingsley; by Thomas Hood who, with financial aid from London magnates, gave lectures at Leadenhall during 1588-96.

These men, along with many others, were protagonists of the view that the intellectual conquest of the oceans must precede their actual conquest. Of this band, John Davis was unique as the first English professional seaman to publish, for the enlightenment of his fellow professionals, a manual of navigation: *The Seamans Secrets* which was first published in 1595 and ran into many editions, the fifth of which was dated 1633. Davis, author of a practical treatise for practical men, was also a visionary who witnessed to navigation as a force at work within the process of history.

> 'And sith Navigation is the meane whereby Countreyes are discovered, and Communitie drawne betweene Nation and Nation, the word of God published to the blessed recovery of the forraine ofcasts from whence it hath pleased his divine Majestie as yet to detaine the brightnesse of his glory: and that by Navigation common-weales through mutuall trade are not onely sufficiently sustained, but mightily enriched with how great esteeme ought the painefull Seaman to be embraced, by whose hard adventures such excellent benefits are achieved, for by his exceeding great hazzards, the forme of the earth, the quantities of Countries, the diversitie of Nations, and the natures of Zones, Climats, Countries and people, are apparantly made knowne unto us.'[17]

The Seamans Secrets, which owes much to Davis's experiences on the northern voyages and the Cavendish voyage, is for us a valuable guide to the state of English navigation in the late Elizabethan age.

The first of its two books is devoted to what he calls 'Horizontall Navigation' or, as we call it, 'plane sailing' which was based on the use of charts which treated the surface of the earth as though it were flat rather than curved and the meridians of longitude as though they were parallel whereas in reality they converge from the equator to the poles. Davis was of course aware of the errors inherent in such a system, but he reckoned it to be adequate over short distances and even over longer ones if the return journey could be made on a reverse track to that of the outward. We are talking of an age in which Mercator's projection which made possible the use on charts of parallel lines to depict the meridians was sufficiently recent (1569) as to be unfamiliar to the vast majority of seamen. In any case, Mercator did not solve the problem of distortion in the high latitudes which interested Davis.

Celestial observation was for Davis an essential ingredient of navigational science. He lists among the instruments 'necessary for the execution of this excellent skill' a cross staff, a quadrant, and an astrolabe and goes on to qualify this statement by citing the cross staff as more reliable than the astrolabe and quadrant for observations at sea. By means of these observations the navigator could identify the latitude of the ship. In the northern hemisphere this was done either by measuring the altitude of the sun at midday (local time) or that of the *Stella Polaris* (the pole star) at night. When the sky was obscured by cloud or fog the navigator was denied access to this priceless information and became perilously dependent upon out-of-date knowledge. It is important in this context to note a serious limitation in sixteenth-century navigational science. There was no practical means of ascertaining the longitude of a ship. This gap was not filled until the perfection of the lunar method and the clock method for so doing in the eighteenth century.

Since the calculation of longitude could be no more than an estimate, the calculation of latitude had to be as accurate as possible. Davis's experiences in the higher latitudes of the Atlantic had given him grounds for unease. The length of summer daylight in these latitudes meant that opportunities for measuring the altitude of *Stella Polaris* might not occur. This put a premium upon accurate observations of the sun. To this end Davis, as he tells us in *The Seamans Secrets*, devised a variant of the cross staff designed to reduce observational errors.[18] This instrument, which came to be known as the back staff (also at a later date the Davis or English quadrant), enabled the observer with his back to the sun to focus upon the horizon and to bring it into line with the shadow cast by the sun. Its advantages were that the observer was spared the glare of the sun and the almost insurmountable difficulty of sighting simultaneously the sun and the horizon. Parallax was also eliminated. The back staff remained in service until its replacement in 1731 by Hadley's reflecting quadrant.

The compass was an indispensable nautical instrument. Davis listed three special things upon which the practice of navigation was grounded, the first of these being the observation of latitude. The second was careful regard 'unto his [the navigator's] steredg, with very diligent examination of the truth of his Compasse, that it bee without variation or other impediments'. Variation, one of many factors productive of errors in navigation, arose out of the inconstant variations between magnetic north and true north which are measured as the angle, either easterly or westerly, between the bearing of the magnetic pole and that of the true pole at the position of the observer. On the eighteenth century charts, lines of equal variation, known as isogonic lines, were drawn for the year of publication. But in Davis's lifetime the navigator had to revise repeatedly his own measurements; for which purpose Davis prescribed as one of his necessary instruments, 'an instrument magneticall', probably an azimuth compass. Variation had to be applied to any course steered by magnetic compass in order to obtain the true course.[19]

The third special thing was 'a careful consideration of the number of leagues that the ship sayleth in every houre or watch, to the neerest estimation that possibly he can give'. There is a puzzle here. Davis sheds no light on how the distance sailed is to be calculated. It may be, though it seems unlikely, that he took for granted that all seamen were so familiar with the use of the log and line for this purpose that it did not require a mention. But this seems at variance with the style and tone of the treatise. A more probable explanation is that *The Seamans Secrets* was, as is suggested by A. H. Markham, editor of Davis's writings, and David Waters, author of *The Art of Navigation in Elizabethan and Early Stuart England,* compiled in a hurry.

All these special things, as Davis called them, are included in a table, we can think of it as a log, printed in the treatise. He urged the seaman to 'keepe his accounts, whereby he may at all times distinctly examine his former practises'. He recommended that every twenty-four hours, measured in nautical fashion from noon to noon, the date, the latitude, the mean course steered, the mean distance run and the wind should be recorded. In a sixth column Davis recorded his measurements of compass variation. In this extract from the log of the *Desire* during her arduous journey home in 1593 from South America, Davis made an important contribution to the standardization of log keeping.[20]

For the majority of late Elizabethan English seamen, knowledge of latitude, calculations, based on use of the traverse board, of the mean course and reckonings of the distance run from the last known or estimated position represented the summit of their technical aspirations. This explains why Davis devoted half of *The Seamans Secrets* to 'Horizontall' navigation, although aware of its weaknesses, and to advice regarding the rise and fall of tides.

The contents of the second book might be described as more theoretical as they advance beyond the techniques of plane sailing and enter into the realms of the paradoxall compass and great circle navigation. Here the practical seaman was invited to face the reality that the earth is a sphere, that the meridians of longitude, far from being parallel, converge upon the poles, and that the shortest distance between two places is not a straight line but the arc of a circle; hence the importance attached by Davis to the globe as both an aid to instruction and an aid to true navigation.

Once again experience, by no means that of Davis alone, of navigation in the high latitudes gained during English searches for northern passages to Asia was a significant factor. The paradoxall compass represented an effort to come to terms with the problems arising therefrom. The term is used only by Dee, who claimed to be its inventor, and Davis, who failed to define it. The evidence available points to the conclusion that the paradoxall compass was in fact a circumpolar chart, having the north pole at its centre, the meridians radiating outwards therefrom in straight lines, and the parallels of latitude shown as concentric circles surrounding the pole.[21] It anticipated modern circumpolar charts designed on the zenithal equidistant projection. Its purpose was to eliminate the gross errors and distortions which were inherent in the use of the plane chart in high latitudes and to find an approximate great circle course. Its use demanded a high degree of skill, especially geometrical skill, which was beyond the scope of most sixteenth century navigators. Things were improved in the seventeenth century through the introduction of the protractor for measuring angles and the publication of tables as an aid to plotting the curved track of the ship.

Davis was familiar with great circle navigation, the chief advantage of which is that the shortest distance between any two places on the earth's spherical surface lies along the great circle which passes through them. This could be found by consulting the globe. To sail the great circle the ship had to make a good curved track over the sea. Adherence to the track necessitated frequent changes of course and the successive courses had to be adhered to strictly. This was the great obstacle to great circle sailing in the days of sail, for, as Davis admitted, the wind direction might at any time create a conflict in the navigator's mind between the prescribed course and that favored by the wind.[22] Great circle navigation became a more practicable proposition with the coming of the steamship and the creation of the gnonomic chart in the nineteenth century.

The Seamans Secrets gives us a good idea of the strengths and limitations of English navigation in the late sixteenth century and of the gaps between theory and practice. Theoretical navigation, as expounded by Davis, outstripped the techniques available. Until Mercator's projection came into general use in the seventeenth century, plane sailing was the usual order of the day. The fact that longitude could not be fixed at sea was a grave limitation. The difficulty of calculating realistically the speed of the ship opened the way to error. Celestial observations might be hampered by the weather and were certainly impeded by the movements of the ship which meant that the observer was operating on an unstable platform. Navigation was subject always to the uncontrollable vagaries of winds and weather. For Davis the disappointment was his failure to sail through the North-west passage. Given that the Arctic seas were impassable in fragile wooden sailing ships, the wonder is not that he failed to break through but that he got as far as he did and lived to bequeath to us so vivid and scientific a testament to the flowering in England of the haven-finding art.

A. N. Ryan, M.A., F.R.Hist.S.
Reader in History, Emeritus
University of Liverpool

NOTES

1. For examples of such confusion, see A. H. Markham (ed.), *The Voyages and Works of John Davies the Navigator*, Hakluyt Society, 1st series, vol. 59 (1880), pp. lxxxviii ff.

2. K. R. Andrews, *Trade, Plunder and Settlement: Maritime Enterprise and the Genesis of the British Empire, 1480-1630* (Cambridge, 1984), pp. 179 ff.; S. E. Morison, *The European Discovery of America: The Northern Voyages, A.D. 500-1600* (New York, 1971), pp. 583.

3. A. H. Markham, *op. cit.*, pp. xi ff. The text of the Letters patent is printed on pp. 368 ff.

4. Davis to Sanderson, 16 September 1587, A. H. Markham, *op. cit.*, p. 59

5. *The Worlde's Hydrographical Description,* A. H. Markham, *op. cit.*, pp. 191 ff.

6. D. B. Quinn (ed.), *The Voyages and Colonising Enterprises of Sir Humphrey Gilbert*, 2 vols., Hakluyt Society, 2nd series, vols. 83-4 (1940) pp. 129 ff.; E. G. R. Taylor, *Tudor Geography* (London, 1930), pp. 34 ff.

7. D. W. Waters, *The Art of Navigation in England in Elizabethan and Early Stuart Times* (London, 1958), pp. 190 ff.

8. A. H. Markham, *op.cit.*, p. 197.

9. *Ibid.*, p. 232.

10. D. B. Quinn (ed.), *The Last Voyage of Thomas Cavendish, 1591-1592: The Autograph Manuscript of his Own Account of the Voyage. Written Shortly before his Death, from the Collection of Paul Mellon* (Chicago and London, 1975), p. 20; S. E. Morison, *The European Discovery of America: The Southern Voyages, A.D. 1492-1616* (New York, 1974), pp. 720 ff.

11. A. H. Markham, *op. cit.*, p. 236.

12. For a convenient survey of Davis's later voyages,

see K.R. Andrews, *op. cit.*, pp. 179 ff. and pp. 263 ff.; A. H. Markham, *op. cit.*, pp. lxiii ff.

13. E. G. R. Taylor (ed.), *A Regiment for the Sea and Other Writings on Navigation by William Bourne of Gravesend a Gunner (c.1535-1582)*. Hakluyt Society, 2nd series, vol. 121 (1963), p. 294.

14. D. W. Waters, *op. cit.*, pp. 26, 86, 87, 626; K. R. Andrews, *op. cit.*, p. 69.

15. D. W. Waters, *op. cit.*, pp. 522.

16. J. W. Shirley, *Thomas Harriot* (New York, 1983) is the standard biography. See also E. G. R. Taylor, 'Hariot's Instructions for Ralegh's Voyage to Guiana, 1595', *Journal of the Institute of Navigation*, vol. V (1952).

17. Extract from the 'Epistle Dedicatorie' (to Charles, Lord Howard of Effingham) of *The Seamans Secrets*. The text of the 1607 edition is printed by A. H. Markham, pp. 229 ff.

18. *The Seamans Secrets*, 1607 ed., pp. 327 ff.

19. E. G. R. Taylor, *The Haven-Finding Art: A History of Navigation from Odysseus to Captain Cook,* 2nd impression (London, 1958), pp. 100 ff., 173 ff., 181 ff., 220 ff.

20. *The Seamans Secrets*, 1607 ed., pp. 281 ff.

21. D. W. Waters, *op. cit.*, pp. 209 ff.

22. *Ibid.*, p. 208.

FURTHER READING

Published Contemporary Writings

A. H. Markham (ed.), *The Voyages and Works of John Davis the Navigator,* Hakluyt Society, 1st series, vol. 59 (1880).

D. B. Quinn (ed.), *The Voyages and Colonising Enterprises of Sir Humphrey Gilbert,* 2 vols., Hakluyt Society, 2nd series, vols. 83-4 (1940). D. B. Quinn (ed.), *The Last Voyage of Thomas Cavendish, 1591-1592: The Autograph Manuscript of His Own Account of the Voyage Written Shortly Before his Death, from the Collection of Paul Mellon* (Chicago and London, 1975). D. B. Quinn (ed.), *New American World: A Documentary History of North America to 1612,* 5 vols. (New York, 1979), vol. iv.

E. G. R. Taylor (ed.), *A Regiment for the Sea and Other Writings on Navigation by William Bourne of Gravesend, a Gunner (c.1535-1582),* Hakluyt Society, 2nd series, vol. 121 (1963).

Modern Publications

K. R. Andrews, *Trade, Plunder and Settlement: Maritime Enterprise and the Genesis of the British Empire, 1480-1630* (Cambridge, 1984).

P. French, *John Dee: The World of an Elizabethan Magus* (London, 1972).

J. B. Hewson, *A History of the Practice of Navigation* (Glasgow, 1951).

R. McIntyre, 'William Sanderson: Elizabethan Financier of Discovery', *William and Mary Quarterly,* vol. 13 (1956).

S. E. Morison, *The European Discovery of America,* vol. 1, *The Northern Voyages, A.D. 500-1600* (New York, 1971).

S. E. Morison, *The European Discovery of America,* vol. 2, *The Southern Voyages, A.D. 1492-1616* (New York, 1974).

D. B. Quinn, *England and the Discovery of America, 1480-1620* (New York, 1974).

D. B. Quinn, *North America from Earliest Discovery to the First Settlements: The Norse Voyages to 1612* (New York, 1978).

J. W. Shirley, *Thomas Harriot* (New York, 1983).

J. W. Shirley (ed.), *Thomas Harriot: Renaissance Scientist* (Oxford, 1974).

E. G. R. Taylor, *Tudor Geography, 1485-1583* (London, 1930).

E. G. R. Taylor, *Late Tudor and Early Stuart Geography, 1583-1650* (London, 1934).

E. G. R. Taylor, *The Mathematical Practitioners of Tudor and Stuart England* (London, 1954).

E. G. R. Taylor, *The Haven-Finding Art: A History of Navigation from Odysseus to Captain Cook,* 2nd impression (London, 1958).

Helen Wallis, 'The First English Globe: A Recent Discovery', *Geographical Journal*, vol. 117 (1951).

Helen Wallis, 'Further Light on the Molyneux Globes', *ibid.*, vol. 121 (1955).

D. W. Waters, *The Art of Navigation in England in Elizabethan and Early Stuart Times* (London, 1958).

DAVIS, JOHN, 1550?-1605.

The seamans secrets. Divided into two parts, wherein is taught the three kindes of sayling, horizontall, paradoxall, and sayling upon a great circle. Also an horizontall tyde-table for the easie finding of the ebbing and flowing of the tydes, with a regiment newly calculated for the finding of the declination of the sunne, and many other most necessary rules and instruments, not heeretofore set forth by any. Newly corrected and amended, and the fifth time imprinted.

London, printed by Iohn Davvson. 1633.

Collation: 21 cm. (4to): A-H^4 ^2A-$^2E^4$ $^2F^2$. [108] p., [1] folded leaf of plates; ill.

Notes: Originally published: London, 1595. Dedication signed (p. [8]): Iohn Davis. "The second part of this treatise of navigation" (p. [65-108]) has special half title leaf and separate signatures.

References: JCB Lib. cat., pre-1675, II, p. 245; STC (2nd ed.), 6371; JCB Lib. *Maritime history*, 77.

JCB Library copy: Acq: 2049. Acquired in 1906. This copy lacks folded leaf of plates; facsimile from the copy in the King's College Library at the University of Cambridge is here inserted. Call number: D633 D268s.

Tracings: 1. Navigation. 2. Nautical instruments. I. Title.

THE SEAMANS SECRETS.

Divided into two parts, wherein is taught the three kindes of Sayling, *Horizontall*, *Paradoxall*, *and Sayling vpon a great Circle.*

Alſo an Horizontall Tyde-Table for the eaſie finding of the ebbing and flowing of the Tydes, with *a Regiment newly calculated for the finding of the* Declination of the Sunne, and many other moſt *neceſſary Rules and Inſtruments, not heeretofore ſet forth by any.*

Newly corrected and amended, and the fifth time Imprinted.

LONDON,
Printed by IOHN DAVVSON.
1633.

To the right honorable Lord *Charles Haward*, Baron of *Effingham*, Knight of the noble order of the Garter, Lieutenant of her *Majesties* Counties of *Sussex* and *Surrey*, Constable of her Majesties *Honour and Castle of* Winsor, *Lord high Admirall of* England, Ireland, *and* Wales, *and* of the Dominions and Isles of the same, of the towne of *Callis* and Marches thereof, *Normandy*, *Gascony*, and *Greynes*, *Captaine generall of her* Majesties *Seas and Navie royall, and one of her* Majesties *most honourable privie Counsell*, John Davis *wisheth increase of honour and perfect felicitie.*

Ight Honourable and my speciall good Lord, as by the instinct of nature, all men are desirous of knowledge, and take pleasure in the varieties of vnderstanding, so it is likewise ingrafted by the same benefit of nature, in the hearts of true nobilitie, not onely to excell the vulgar sort, but also to cherish, support, and countenance all such as shall in due course prosecute their vocatiō; and as such practises either speculatiue or mechanicall, shall receiue favourable place in the honorable opinion of nobilitie, by so much the more shall the practiser be esteemed: which is the cause that at this time imboldeneth me to present vnto your most honourable favour this small Treatise of Navigation, being a briefe collection of such practises as in my severall Voyages I haue from experience collected. Among which in three severall attempts for the discovery of the Northwest passage, thereby to find a short & navigable course vnto the rich and famous Countries of *Cathayo, China, Pegu*, the Isles *Moluccan* and *Philipina*, that therby to the great and inestimable benefit of our Countrey, there might be a rich and plentifull trade procured betweene vs and the said Nations, in short time to be performed, and with great safetie in regard of the course: which action and discovery (by meanes of that honourable Counseller Sir *Francis Walsingham* Knight, principall Secretarie to her *Majestie*) was with good resolution accepted by the Marchants of London, but in the decay of his honourable life, the attempt was likewise quailed: but howsoever mens mindes alter, yet vndoubtedly, there is passage navigable, and easie to be performed by that course (whensoever it shall please God to reveale the same) by invincible reasons and sufficient experience to be proved: and although before I entred into that discovery, I was sufficiently perswaded of the certaintie thereof, by historicall relation, substantially confirmed, whereof to the Adventurers I made sufficient proofe, but especially to my worshipfull good friend Maister *William Sanderson*, the onely Marchant that to his great charges, with most cōstant travaile, did labour for the finishing thereof: yet I thanke God that of late it hath beene my very good chance, to receiue better assurance then ever before of the certaintie of that passage, and such was my vehement desire for the performance thereof, that thereby I was onely induced to goe with M: *Candish* in his second attempt for the South Seas, vpon his constant promise vnto me, that when we came to the *California*, I should there haue his Pinnice with my owne Bark (which for that purpose went with me to my great charges) to search that Northwest discovery vpon those backe parts of *America*, but God hath otherwise disposed our purposes in his divine Iudgements, for Maister *Candish* being halfe way through the straights of *Magilane*, and impatient of the tempestuous furiousnesse of that place, having all his Shippes and company with him, returned for *Brasil*, by the authoritie of his command, when with a leading wind wee might haue passed the same, and returning

more

more then 80. leagues toward *Brasil*, my selfe being in his Ship named the *Desire*, without Boate, Oares, Sayles, Cables, cordage, victuals, or health of my company sufficient for that attempt, was separated in a freit of weather, and forced to seeke the next shore for my reliefe, and recovering a harborow by vs named *Port Desire*, being in the latitude of 48. deg. did there repaire my most miserable wants, and there staying foure moneths in most lamentable distresse, did againe conclude with my company, to giue another attempt to passe the straights, as my best meane to gaine reliefe. And three times I was in the South Seas, but still by furious weather forced backe againe: yet notwithstanding all this my labour to performe the Voyage to his profite, and to saue my selfe (for I did adventure and my good friends for my sake 1100. pounds in the action) M. *Candish* was content to account me to be the author of his overthrow, and to write with his dying hand that I ranne from him, when that his owne Ship was returned many moneths before me.

I am bold to make this relation vnto your Lordship, onely to satisfie your Honor of my conversation, for were I faultie of so foule a crime, I were worthy of ten thousand torments, in presuming to present this Treatise to your honourable Lordship, and now referring my cause to your Lordships consideration, I will againe returne to my purpose.

In those Northwest voyages, where Navigation must be executed in most exquisite sort, in those attempts I was enforced to search all possible meanes required in sayling, by which occasion I haue gathered together this briefe Treatise, which with my selfe I doe dedicate to your honourable protection, being desirous if it lay in my power to doe farre greater matters in your Lordships service, hoping of your honourable pardon, because it is onely done to shew my dutifull affection, & not for any singularitie that the worke containeth. For I thinke there bee many hundreds in England that can in a farre greater measure and more excellent methode expresse the noble art of Navigation, and I am fully perswaded that our Countrey is not inferiour to any for men of rare knowledge, singular explication, and exquisite execution of the Arts Mathematicke, for what strangers may be compared with M. *Thomas Digges* Esquire, our Countryman the great Maister of Archmastrie, and for Theoricall speculations and most cunning calculation, M. *Dee* and M. *Thomas Heriotts* are hardly to be matched: and for the mechanicall practises drawne from the Arts of Mathematicke, our Countrey doth yeeld men of principall excellencie, as M. *Emery Mulleneax* for the exquisite making of Globes-bodies, and M. *Nicholas Hellyar* for the singularitie of portraiture, haue the praise of Europe, M. *Baker* for his skill and surpassing grounded knowledge for the building of Ships advantageable to all purposes, hath not in any Nation his equall.

And now that I may returne to the painefull Seaman, it is not vnknowne to all Nations of the earth, that the English goeth before all others in the practises of sayling, as appeareth by the excellent discovery of Sir *Francis Drake* in his passage through the straights of *Magilane*, which being then so rashly knowne, he could not haue passed, vnlesse he had bin a man of great practise and rare resolution: so much I may boldly say, because I haue seene & tasted the frowardnesse of the place, with the great vnlikelihood of any passage to be that way.

I might here repeate the most valiant & excellent attempts of Sir *Hugh Willoughbie*, Sir *Iohn Hawkins*, Sir *Humphry Gilbert*, and your Lordships servant M. *George Raymond*, with divers others that haue given most resolute attempts in the practises of Navigation, aswell for the discouery as other execution, whereby good proofe is made, that not onely in the skill of Navigation, but also in the mechanicall execution of the practises of sayling, wee are not to be matched by any Nation of the earth.

And sith Navigation is the meane whereby Countryes are discovered, and communitie drawne betweene Nation and Nation, the word of God published to the blessed recovery of the forraine ofcasts from whence it hath pleased his divine Majestie as yet to detaine the brightnesse of his glory: and that by Navigation common-weales through mutuall trade are not onely sufficiently susteined, but mightily enriched with how great esteeme ought the painefull Seaman to be embraced, by whose hard adventures such excellent benefits are atchieved, for by his exceeding great hazzards, the forme of the earth, the quantities of Countries, the diversitie of Nations, and the natures of Zones, Climats, Countries and people, are apparantly made knowne vnto vs. Besides, the great benefits mutually interchanged betweene Nations, of such fruits, commodities, and artificiall practises wherewith God hath blessed each particular country, coast, and nation, according to the nature and scituation of the place.

For what hath made the *Spanyard* to be so great a Monarch, the Commander of both *Indias*, to abound in wealth and all natures benefits, but onely the painefull industrie of his Subjects in Navigation, their former trade was only figs, oringes, and oyle, but now through Navigation is brought to be gold, silver, pearles, silkes, and spice, by long and painefull trade recovered. Which great benefits onely by her *Majesties* loving clemency & mercifull favour he doth possesse: for if her Highnes and her most honourable Lords would not regard the small distance betweene her dominions and those famous rich Kingdomes, the easinesse of the passage being once discovered (the Northwest I meane) with the full sufficiencie of her Highnes Subjects to effect the same, there could then be no doubt, but her stately seat of *London* should be the storehouse of *Europe*, & a nurse to all Nations, in yeelding all Indian commodities in a farre better condition, and at a more easie rate then now brought vnto vs, exchanging commodities of our owne store, with a plentifull returne at the first hand, which now by many exchanges are brought vnto vs.

Then should the *Spanyard* againe returne to his olde trade, and our sacred Soveraigne be seated the Commander of the earth: which trade and most fortunate discovery, we aboue all nations ought most principally to regard, because of the singularitie and invincible force of our Shipping, which is not onely the commanding Fortresse of our Countrey, but also the dread of our adversary, and the glory of our nation: wherein we doe in no sort flatter our selues, for it was made apparant to all Nations of the earth, by the late most famous conquest that her *Maiesty* had against the huge supposed invincible fleete of the *Spanyard*, being by her Navy vnder the command of your Lordship, who there in person & in place of her *Maiestie*, to your eternall glorious fame did disgrace their glory and confound their force, aud manifest their weaknesse by their dastardly flight, through Gods providence and your Lordships stately resolution.

Then sith Navigation is a matter of so great moment, I suppose that every man is bound in duty to giue his best furtherance thereunto: among whom as the most vnmeete of all, yet wishing all good to the painefull traveller, I haue published this short Treatise, naming it the *Seamans Secrets*, because by certaine questions demaunded and answered, I haue not omitted any thing that appertaineth to the secret of Navigation, whereby if there may grow any increase of knowledge or ease in practise it is the thing which I chiefly desire.

To manifest the necessary conclusions of Navigation in briefe and short tearmes, is my onely intent, and therefore I omit to declare the causes of tearmes and definition of artificiall wordes, as matter superfluous to my purpose, neither haue I layde downe the cunning conclusions apt for Schollers to practise vpon the shore, but onely those things that are needfully required in a sufficient Seaman: beseeching your honourable Lordship to pardon my boldnesse, and with your favourable countenance to regard my dutifull affection, I most humbly commit your good Lordship to the mercies of God, who long preserue your health, with continuall increase of honour.

From *Sandrudge* by *Darthmouth* the 20. of August. 1594.

Your Lordships in all dutifull seruice to commaund,

JOHN DAVIS.

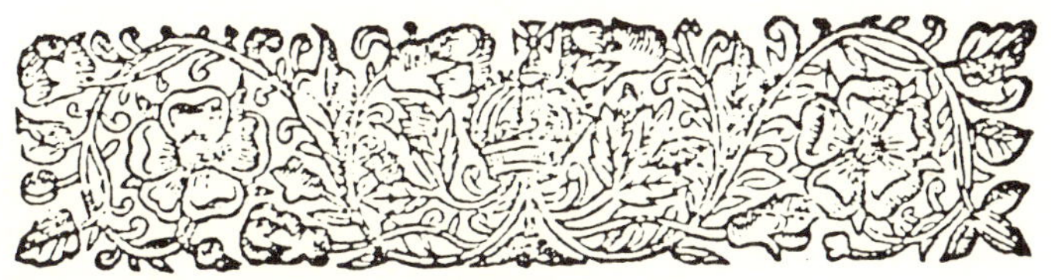

THE FIRST BOOKE OF THE *SEAMANS SECRETS.*

What is Navigation?

Avigation is that excellent Art which demonstrateth by infallible conclusions, how a sufficient Ship may bee conducted the shortest good way from place to place, by Corse and Trauers.

What are these infallible conclusions?

NAvigation consisteth of three parts, which being well understood and practised, are conclusions infallible, whereby the skilfull Pilote is void of all doubt to effect the thing purposed. Of which, the first is the Horizontall Nauigation, which manifesteth all the varieties of the Ships motion within the Horizontall plaine superficies, where every line drawne is supposed a parallell.

The second is a paradoxall or Cosmographicall Nauigation, which demonstrateth the true motion of the ship upon any course assigned in longitude, latitude, and distance, either particular or generall, and is the skilfull gathering together of many Horizontall Corses, into one infallible and true motion paradoxall.

The third is great circle Nauigation, which teacheth how vpon a great Circle drawne betweene any two places assigned, (being the onely shortest way betweene place and place) the Shippe may be conducted, and is performed by the skilfull application of Horizontall and paradoxall Nauigation.

What is a Corse?

A Corse is that paradoxall line which passeth betweene place and place, according to the true Horizontall position of the Magnet, vpon which line the Ship prosecuting her motion, shall be conducted betweene the said places.

What is a Trauers?

A Trauers is the varietie or alteration of the Shippes motion vpon the shift of windes within any Horizontall plaine superficies, by the good collection of which Trauerses, the Ships vniforme motion or Corse is giuen.

What Instruments are necessary for the execution of this excellent skill?

The Instruments necessary for a skilfull Seaman, are a Sea Compasse, a Crosse staffe, a Quadrant, an Astrolaby, a Chart, an Instrument magneticall for the finding of the variation of the Compasse, an Horizontall plaine Sphere, a Globe, and a paradoxall Compasse. By which instruments, all conclusions and infallible demonstrations, Hidrographicall, Geographicall, and Cosmographicall, are without controlement of errour to be performed: but the Sea Compasse, Chart, and Crosse staffe, are instruments sufficient for the Seamans vse: the Astrolabie and Quadrant being instruments very vncertaine for Sea obseruations.

What

What is the Sea Compaſſe?

THe Sea Compaſſe, is a principall inſtrument in Nauigation repreſenting and diſtinguiſhing the Horizon, ſo that the Compaſſe may conueniently be named an Artificiall Horizon, becauſe by it are manifeſted all the limits and diſtinctions of the Horizon required to the perfect vſe of Nauigation, which diſtinctions are the 32. points of the Compaſſe, whereby the Horizon is diuided into 32 equall parts, and euery of thoſe poynts hath his proper name, as in the figure following appeareth. Alſo euery point of the Compaſſe doth containe degrees, minuts, ſeconds, & thirds, &c. Which degrees are called degrees of Azumuth, whereof there are in euery point $11\frac{1}{4}$. ſo that the whole Compaſſe or Horizon containeth 360. degrees of Azumuth, for if you multiply $11\frac{1}{4}$. degrees, the degrees that each point containeth, by 32. the points of the Compaſſe it yeeldeth 360. the degrees of the Compaſſe. And of minutes each point containeth 45 being $\frac{3}{4}$. of an houre, ſo that the whole Compaſſe is hereby diuided into 24. houres, by which accompt there are in an houre 15. degrees, ſo that euery degree containeth 4. minutes of time, for an houre conſiſting of 60. minutes hath for his fifteenth part 4 minutes of time, and in euery minute there is ſixtie ſeconds, and euery ſecond containeth ſixtie thirds, either in degrees applyed to time, or degrees applied to meaſure: ſo that the generall content of the Compaſſe is 32. points, 360. degrees, and 24. houres with their minutes, ſeconds, and thirds.

What is the vſe of the 32. points of the Compaſſe?

THe vſe of the 32. points of the Compaſſe, is to direct the skilfull Pilote by Horizontall trauers, how he may conclude the corſe or paradoxall motion of his Ship, thereby with the greater expedition to recouer the place deſired, becauſe they diuide the horizon in ſuch limits as are moſt apt for Nauigation, they doe alſo diſtinguiſh the windes by their proper names, for the winde receiueth his name by that part of the horizon from whence it bloweth.

What is the vse of 360. degrees of Azumuth?

By the degrees of Azumuth is knowne the quantity of the rising and setting of the Sunne, Moone, and Starres, whereby is knowne the length of the dayes and nights in all climates, and at all times, they also shew a most precise Horizontall distinction of the motion of the Sunne, Moone, and Starres, whereby the certaintie of time is measured, and the variation of the Compasse, with the Poles height, is ingeniously knowne at all times and in all places by the helpe of the Globe.

How is the houre of the day knowne by the Compasse?

IT hath beene an ancient custome among Mariners to diuide the Compasse into 24. equall parts or houres, by which they haue vsed to distinguish time, supposing an East Sunne to be 6. of the clocke, a Southeast Sunne 9. of the clocke, and a South Sunne 12. of the clocke, &c. as in the figure following shall plainly appeare. But this account is very absurd, for with vs in England (the Sunne hauing his greatest North declination,) it is somewhat past 7 of the clocke, at an East Sunne, and at a Southeast Sunne it is past 10. of the clocke: also when the Sunne is in the Equinoctiall, the Sunne is halfe the day East, and halfe the day West, to all those that be vnder the same, so that the Sunne then and to those people vseth but two points of the Compasse, to performe the motion of 12. houres: therefore the distinctions of time may not well be giuen by the Compasse, vnlesse the Sunne be vpon the Meridian, or that you be farre toward the North, in such places where the Sunnes Horizontall motion is very oblique, for there the houre may be giuen by the Compasse, without any great errour, but else-where it cannot. Therefore those that trauaile must either vse the Globe, or an Equinoctiall Diall, by whom time may be most certainly measured, if there be good consideration of the variation of the Needle, by which the Equinoctiall Diall is directed, for this is a generall thing to be regarded, as well in the Compasse, as in any dials or other instrument, or conclusion whatsoeuer, wherein the vse of the Needle is required, that vnlesse there be good regard vnto the variation of the same, there can no good conclusion follow of any such practises.

What

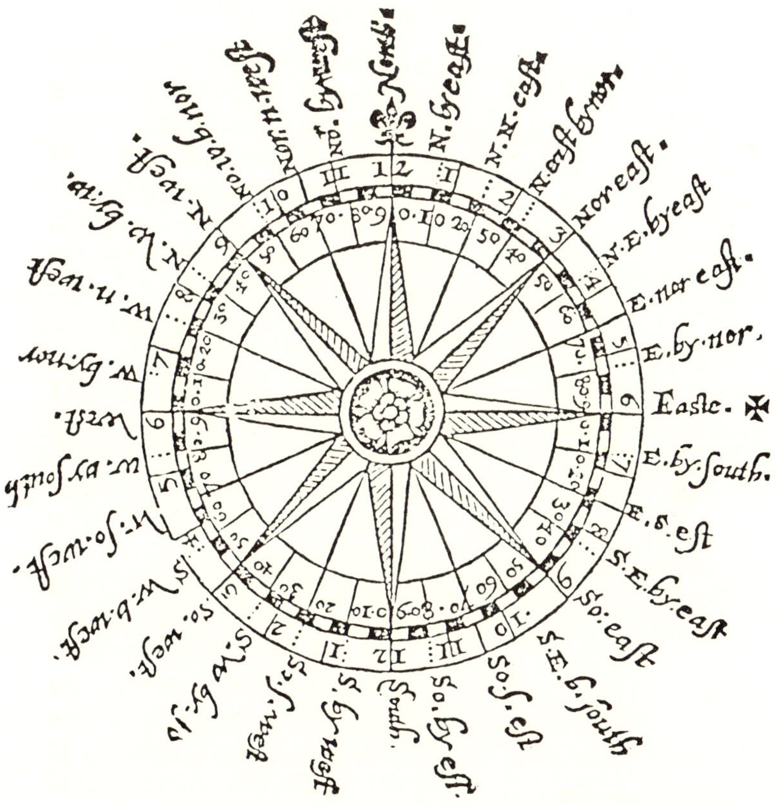

What is the next neceſſary thing to be learned?

Hauing perfectly learned the compaſſe, the next neceſſary thing for a Seaman to know, is the alteration or ſhifting of tydes that thereby he may with the greater ſafetie bring his ſhip into any barred port, hauen, creeke, or other place, where tydes are to be regarded. And this difference of tydes in the alteration of flowing and reflowing, is by long experience found to be gouerned by the Moones motion, for in ſuch proportion of time as the Moone doth ſeparate her ſelfe from the Sunne, by the ſwiftnes of her naturall motion: in the like proportion of time doth one tyde differ

 from

from another, therefore to understand this difference of the Moones motion, is the onely meane whereby the time of tyde is most precisely knowne

Of the Moones Motion.

YOu must understand the Moone hath two kindes of motions, a naturall motion, and a violent motion, her violent motion is from the East toward the West, caused by the violent swiftnes of the diurnall motion of primū mobile, in which motion the moone is carried about the earth in 24. houres and 50. minutes neerest one day with another, for although the diurnall period of the first mouer be performed in 24. houres, yet because the Moone every day in her slowest naturall motion moueth 12 degrees, therefore shee is not carried about the earth, untill that her motion be also carried about, which is in 24. houres and 50. minutes neerest.

Her naturall motion is from the West towards the East, contrary to the motion of the first mouer, wherein the Moone hath three differences of mouing, a swift motion, a meane motion, & a slow motion, all which is performed by the divine ordinance of the Creator in 27. dayes and 8. houres, neerest through all the degrées of the Zodiac.

Her slow motion is in the point of Auge or apogeo, being then farthest distant from the earth, and then she moueth in every day 12. degrees.

Her swift motion is in the opposite of Auge or perigeo, being neerest unto the earth, at which time shee moueth 14. degrees, with some small difference of minutes in every 24. houres.

Betweene those two points is her meane motion, and then she moueth 13. degrées néerest: all which differences are caused by the excentricitie of hee Orbe wherein shée moueth, and are onely performed in the Zodiac, but the Seamen for their better ease in the knowledge of the tydes, haue applyed this the Moones motion to the points, degrees, & minutes of the Compasse, whereby they haue framed it to bée an Horizontall motion, which sith by long practise is found to be a rule of such certaintie, as that the errour thereof bringeth no danger to the expert Seaman, therefore it is not amisse to follow their practised precepts therein.

In

In euery 29 dayes 12. houres 44 minuts with another through the yeare, the Sunne and Moone are in coniunction, and therfore that is the quantitie of time betwéene change and change, for although the Moone in 27. dayes and 8. houres, performing her naturall motion, doth returne to the same minute of the Zodiac from whence she departed, yet being so returned, shee doth not finde the Sunne in that part of the Ecliptick where shee left him, for the Sunne in his naturall motion mouing euery day one degree towards the East, is moued so far from the place where the Moone left him, as that the Moone cannot ouertake the Sunne to come in coniunction with him, vntil she haue performed the motion of 2. dayes, 4 houres, and 44. minutes néerest, more then her naturall reuolution, and that is the cause wherefore there are 29. dayes, 12. houres, 44. minutes betweene change and change one with another through the whole yeare: but the Seaman accompteth the Moones motion to be vniforme in all places of the Zodiac alike, limitting her generall separation from the Sunne to be such as is her slowest naturall motion, which is 12. degrees, or 48. minutes of time, in euery 24. houres.

By which accompt there are 30. dayes reckoned betwéene change and change, being 11. houres, 16. minuts, more then in truth there is: but because this difference breedeth but small errour in their accompt of tydes, therefore to alter practised Rules where there is no vrgent cause, were a matter friuolous, which considered, I thinke it not amisse that we proceed therein by the same method that commonly is exercised.

Allowing the Moone in euery 24. houres, to depart from the Sunne 12. degrees, or 48 minutes of time, and in this separation the Moone moueth from the Sunne Eastward, vntill shee be at the full, for betweene the change & the full, it is called the Moones separation from the Sunne: for after the full shee doth apply towards the Sunne, so that betweene the full and the change, it is called the Moones application to the Sunne, in which time of application she is to the Westward of the Sunne, as in her separation she is to the Eastward, or I may say in the Seamans phrase all the time of her application she is before the Sunne, and in the time of her separation she is abaft the Sunne.

Then if the Moone doe moue 48. minuts of time in 24. houres

is

it followeth that she doth moue 24. minutes in 12. houres, and in 6. houres she moueth 12. minutes, therefore euery houre she moueth 2. minutes, and such as is the difference of her motion such is the alteration of tydes, and therfore euery tyde differeth from the other 12. minutes, because there is 6. houres betwéene tyde and tyde: and in euery houre the course of flowing or reflowing altereth 2. minutes, whereby it appeareth that in 24. houres the foure tydes of flowing and reflowing doe differ 48 minutes of time.

And sith the whole knowledge of this difference or alteration of tydes, as also the quantitie of the Moones separation and application to and from the Sunne, dependeth vpon the knowledge of the Moones age, it is therefore necessary, that next you learne how the Sunne may be knowne.

For the performance whereof there are two numbers especially required, named the Prime and the Epact, for by the Prime the Epact is found, and by helpe of the Epact the Moones age is knowne.

Of the prime or Golden number.

The prime is the space of 19 yeares, in which time the Moone performeth all the varieties of her motion with the Sunne, and at the end of 19. yeares beginneth the same reuolution againe therefore the prime neuer exceedeth the number of 19. and this prime doth alwayes begin in January, and thus the prime is found: vnto the yeare of the Lord wherein you desire to know the prime, adde 1. then diuide that number by 19. and the remaining number which commeth not into the quotient is the prime. Example in the yeare of our Lord 1590. I desire to know the prime, therefore I adde 1. vnto that yeare, and then it is 1591. which I diuide by 19. and it yéeldeth in the quotient 83. and there remaineth 14. vpon the diuision, which commeth not into the quotient, which 14. is the prime in the yeare of our Lord. 1590.

```
1590              1
   1              4
----            7 7 4
1591          x 5 9 x (83
                x 9 9
                  x
```

The

The Epact is a number proceeding from the overplus of the solar and lunar yeare which number never exceedeth 30. because the Moones age never exceedeth 30 for the finding whereof this number onely serveth: and thus the Epact is knowne, which Epact doth allwayes begin in March, multiply the prime by 11. (being the neerest difference betweene the solar and lunar yeare) divide the product by 30. and the remainer is the Epact. Example in the yeare of our Lord 1590. I would know the Epact, first I seeke the prime of that yeare, and find it to be 14 I therefore multiplie 14 by 11. and that yeeldeth 154 which being divided by 30. it giveth the quotent 5. and there remaineth 4 upon the division, which 4. is the Epact in the yeare 1590. which beginning in March, doth continue untill the next March of the yeare 1591.

14
11
—
14
14
—
154

x 5 (4(5
30

Of the solar and lunar yeare.

The solar yeare or the Suns yeare consisteth of 12. moneths, being 365 dayes, and about 6. houres, the lunar yeare or the Moones yeare containeth 12. Moones, and every Moone hath 29. dayes 12. houres, 44. minutes neerest, which amount unto 354 dayes, 5 houres, 28. minutes, the content of the lunar yeare, which being substracted from 365. dayes 6. houres, there resteth 11. dayes and 23 minutes, the difference betweene the said yeares, from which difference the Epact commeth.

By this Table the Prime and Epact may for euer be found, for when the yeeres be expired, you may begin againe and continue it for euer at your pleasure.

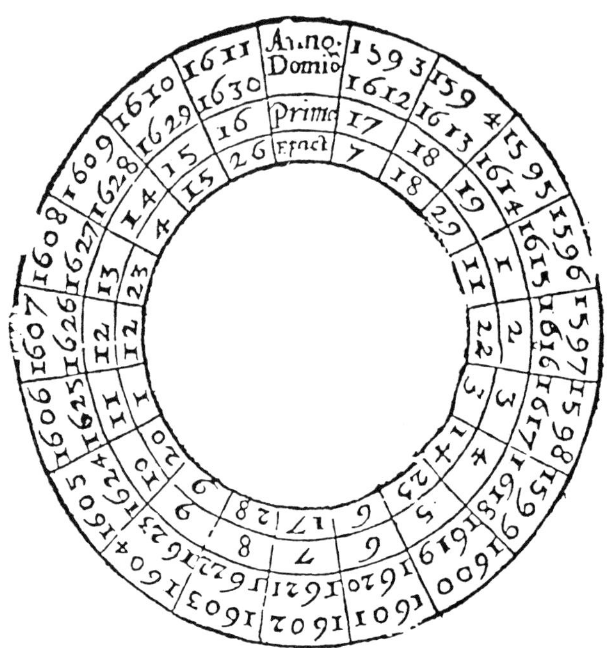

The first circle containeth the yeares of our Lord, the second the prime, and the third and inner circle sheweth the Epact: vnder euery yeare you shall finde his prime and Epact, the prime beginneth in January, and the Epact in March.

How to finde out the Moones age.

The number of moneths

First consider the day of the moneth wherein you seeke the Moones age, then note how many moneths there are betweene the sayd moneth and March, including both moneths, vnto those numbers adde the Epact of that yeare, that is, you must adde into one summe the day of the moneth, betweene March, & your moneth recko-

reckoning both moneths and the Epact, all which numbers ioyned together, if they exceed not 30. is the Moones age, if they be more then 30. cast away 30. as often as you can, and the remainer is the Moones age, if it be iust 30. it is then new Moone, if 7. it is the first quarter day, if 15 it is full Moone, if 22. it is then the last quarter day, and thus the Moones age is found for euer.

And now being able for all times either past, present, or to come, to giue the Moones age, I thinke it good by a few questions conuenient for the Seamans practice, to make you understand the necessary use thereof.

For the accouat of Tydes.

VVHen you desire to know the time of full Sea in any place at all such seasons as occasiō shall require, you must first learne what Moone maketh a full Sea in the same place, that is, upon what poynt of the Compasse the Moone is, when it is full Sea at the said place, you must also know what houre is appropriated to that point of the Compasse, as before is shewed: for upon the change day it will alwayes be full Sea in that place, at the same instant of time, by which considerations you must thus proceede for the search of tydes.

Multiplie the Moones age by 4 diuide the product by 5. and to the quotient adde the houre, which maketh full Sea in that place upon the change day, if it exceede 12. cast away 12. as oft as you may, and then the houre of full Sea remaineth, and for euery 1. that resteth upon your diuision, allow 12. minutes to be added to the houres, for 2. 24. minutes, for 3. 36. and for 4. 48. minutes, for more then 4. will neuer remaine, & thus you may know your Tydes to a minute, example, the Moone being twelue dayes old, I desire to know the time of full Sea at London: first it is found by experience, that a Southwest & Northeast Moone makes full Sea at London, next I consider that 3. of the clocke is the houre appropriated to that point of the Compasse, which number I kéepe in memorie, then I multiply the Moones age, being 12. by 4. and that yéeldeth 48. which being diuided by 5 it giueth in the quotient 9. and 3, remaineth, I adde the quotient 9. to the houre 3. and it maketh 12, houres, and for the remaining number 3. I also adde

46. minutes, so that I finde when the Moone is 12. dayes olde, it is 12. of the clocke and 36. minuts past, at the instant of the full Sea at London: by this order you may at all places and times know the certaintie of your tydes at your pleasure.

But those that are not practised in Arithmeticke, may account these tydes in this sort, knowing how many dayes old the Moone is, he must place the Moone upon that point of the Compasse which maketh full Sea at the place desired, and then reckoning from that point with the Sunne according to the diurnall motion must account so many poynts, and so many times 3. minutes as the Moone is dayes old, that is, for every day one point and three minuts, and there finding the Sunne, he must consider what is the houre allowed to that point where he findeth the Sunne, for that is the houre of full Sea. As for Example, the Moone being 12. dayes old, I desire to know the houre of full Sea at London, now finding by former experience, that a Southwest Moone maketh full Sea at London, I therefore place the Moone upon the point Southwest, then I account from the point Southwest 12. points reckoning with the Sunne according to the diurnall motion, Southwest and by west for the first point, West Southwest for the second, West by South for the third West for the fourth point, and so forth, untill I come to North, which is 12. points from the Southwest, and because the Moone moveth 3. minutes more then a poynt in every day, I therefore adde 3. times twelve, which make 36 minuts to the point North, at which place I find the Sunne to be, and knowing that 12. of the clocke is appropriated to the point North. I may therefore boldly say that at twelve of the clocke 26. minutes past, it is full Sea at London, when the Moone is twelve dayes olde, which 36. minutes are added, because the Moone hath moved 36. minutes more then 12. poynts in those 12 dayes, which is one poynt and 3. minutes for every day, as before.

Here followeth a very necessary Instrument for the knowledge of the Tydes, named *an Horizontall Tyde-Table.*

Of

Of this Instrument and his parts.

This necessary instrument for the young practising Seamans vse, named an Horizontall Tyde-Table, whereby he may shift his Sunne and Moone (as they terme it) and know the time of his tydes with ease and very certainely, (besides the answering of many pleasant and necessary questions vsed amongst Mariners) I haue contriued into this methode, onely for the benefite of such yong practisers in Nauigation.

The first part of this Instrument is a Sea Compasse, diuided into 32. poynts or equall partes the innermost circle of which Compasse is diuided into 24. houres, and euery of those into 4. quarters, each quarter being 15. minutes and against euery point of the Compasse those places are layde downe, in which places it is full Sea when the Moone commeth vpon the same poynt, so that whatsoeuer is required as touching time, or the points of the Compasse is there to be knowne.

The next moueable circle vpon this Compasse, is limited to the Sunne, vpon whose Index the Sunne is layd downe, which circle is diuided into 30. equall parts or dayes, signifying the 30. dayes betwéene change and change, according to the Seamans account so that whatsoeuer is demanded as touching the age of the Moon, is vpon that circle to be knowne.

The vppermost moueable circle is applyed to the Moone, vpon whose Index the Moone is layd downe, which is to be placed either to the points and partes of the Compasse, or to the time of her age, as the question requireth, which considered, the vse of this Instrument is largely manifested, by these questions with their answers following.

How to know the houre of the night by the Moone, being vpon any poynt of the Compasse by this Instrument.

1. Q. The Moone 10. dayes old, I demand what is a clocke, when she is East Northeast?

1. A. In this question the Moones age and the poynt of the Compasse is giuen, thereby to know the houre, I therefore place

 the

the index of the Moone vpon the point East Northeast, there keeping the same not to be moued, then because the moone is 10. daies olde, I moue the Index of the Sunne vntill I bring the 10. day of the moones age vnto the Index of the moone, and there I looke by the Index of the Sunne, and find vpon the Compasse that it is twelue of the clocke at noone & 30. minuts past, when the moone is vpon the poynt East Northeast, being 10. dayes olde.

2. Q. The Moone being twelue dayes olde, I demand at what houre she will be vpon the poynt S. S. E?

2. A. In this question the point of the Compasse and Moones age is giuen as in the first, therefore I place the Index of the Moone vpon the point S. S. E. And there holding it without mouing I turne the Index of the Sunne, vntill the twelfth day of the moones age come to the Index of the Moone, and then the Index of the Sunne sheweth me vpon the Horizon the houre 8 therefore I say that at 8. of the clocke at night, the Moone was then vpon the poynt South Southeast

And thus you may at all times know the houre of the night by the Moone, vpon any poynt of the Compasse, so that the moones age be also had.

How by this Instruction, you may know at all times vpon what point of the Compasse the Moone is.

1. Q. When the Moone is 10. dayes olde vpon what point of the Compasse shall she be at 9. of the clocke in the morning?

1. A. In this question the houre of the day and the moones age is giuen, thereby to finde vpon what poynt of the Compasse she is at the same time. I therefore place the Index of the Sunne vpon the Compasse, at the houre 9. of the clocke in the morning, being vpon the poynt Southeast, then I turne the Index of the Moone vntill I bring it to the tenth day of her age, and then I see vpon the Compasse, that the moone is North and by East, and 15 min. to the Eastwards, of 9. of the clocke when she is 10. dayes olde.

2. Q. When the moone is 20. dayes olde, vpon what point of the Compasse will she be at 2. of the clocke in the afternoone?

2. A. I place the Index of the Sunne vpon the houre 2. noted in the Compasse, there holding the same without mouing, then I

turne

Turne the Index of the Moone, untill I bring it unto the 20. day of her age, and there I see upon the Compasse that shee is Northeast and by north, and 15 minutes to the north-ward, at 2. of the clocke in the afternoone, when she is 20. dayes old.

To finde the Moonesage by this Instrument.

1. Q. When the Moone is North at 7. of the clocke in the afternoone, how old is she?

1. A, In this question the point of the Compasse and the houre is giuen, for the finding of the Moones age: therefore I set the Index of the Sunne upon the houre 7. in the forenoone, there holding it without mouing, then I bring the Index of the Moone to the poynt North and then upon the circle containing the dayes of the Moones age, I see the Moone is 8 dayes and about 18. houres old, when she is North at 7. of the clocke in the forenoone.

2. Q When the Sunne is East and the Moone Southeast, how old is the Moone?

2. A. In this question the points of the Compasse are onely giuen for the finding of the Moones age, therefore I set the Index of the Sunne upon the point East, there holding him steadie, then I put the Index of the Moone upon the poynt Southwest, and there I see that the Moone is 18. dayes and 18. houres olde, when the Sunne is East and shee Southwest.

After this order by the varietie of these few questions, you may frame unto your selfe many other pleasant and necessary questions, which are very easily answered by this Instrument: and entring into the reasons of their answers, you may very readily by a little practise, be able by memorie to answer all such questions with ease.

How to know the time of your tydes by this Instrument.

1. Q. When the Moone is 12. dayes olde, I desire to know the time of full Sea at London

1. A. To answer this question, I first looke through all the poynts of the Compasse of my Instrument, untill I finde where London is written, for when the Moone commeth upon the point

of the Compasse, it will then be full sea at London: therefore I place the Index of the Moone upon the same poynt, which I finde to be Southwest or Northeast, there holding the Index not to be moued, then I turne the Index of the Sunne vntill I bring the twelfth day of the Moones age to the Index of the Moone, and then the Index of the Sunne sheweth me that at 12. of the clocke 36. minutes past it is full sea at London, the Moone being 12. dayes olde.

2. Q. The Moone being 21. dayes olde, at what time is it full Sea at Dartmouth?

2. A. I finde vpon my Instrument that Dartmouth is noted vpon the poynts East and West, whereby I know that when the Moone is East or West it is allwayes full sea at Dartmouth: therefore I place the Index of the Moone vpon the poynt East, and there holding it without mouing, I turne the Index of the Sunne, vntill I bring the 21. day of the Moones age vnto the Index of the Moone, and then the Index of the Sunne sheweth mee vpon the Compasse, that at 10. of the clocke and 48 minuts past, it is full sea at Dartmouth, when the Moone is 21. dayes olde, and not onely at Dartmouth, but my Instrument sheweth mee that at the same instant it is also full sea at Exmouth, Weymouth Plymouth, Mounts bay, at Linne, and at Humber: and thus with great facilitie the time of flowings and reflowings is most precisely knowne.

And now that there may be a finall end of the vses and effects of the Compasse, it is conuenient that I make knowne vnto you, how many leagues shall be sayled vpon euery particular poynt of the Compasse, for the raising or laying of the degrees of latitude, and in the distance sayling how farre you shall be separated from the Meridian from whence the said courses are begun, for as euery poynt of the Compasse hath his certaine limited distance for the degrées of the Poles eleuation, so doe they likewise lead from longitude to longitude, euery poynt according to his ratable limits, which distances of leagues are without alteration, kéeping one and the same proportion in euery particular Horizon of any latitude, but the degrées of longitude answerable to such distances, doe differ in euery altitude, according to the nature of the parallel, as hereafter shall be more plainely manifested. And now

knew,

know that in ſayling North and South, you depart not from your Meridian, and in every 20. leagues ſayling you raiſe a degree: North and by East raiſeth a degree in ſayling 20. leagues and one mile, and leadeth from the Meridian 4. leagues: Nor noreaſt raiſeth a degree in ſayling 21. leagues and two miles, leadeth from the Meridian 8. leagues and one mile: Noreaſt by north raiſeth a degree in ſayling 24. leagues, and leadeth from the Meridian 13. leagues and a mile: Noreaſt raiſeth a degree in ſayling 28 leagues and a mile, and leadeth from the Meridian 20 leagues: Noreaſt by eaſt raiſeth a degree in ſayling 36. leag. and leadeth from the Meridian 30. leagues: Eaſt noreaſt raiſeth a degree in ſayling 52 leagues and a mile and leadeth from the Meridian 48 leagues and 2. miles: Eaſt and by north raiſeth a degree in ſayling 102 leagues and a mile, and leadeth from the Meridian 100 leagues and 2 miles: Eaſt and Weſt doe not raiſe or lay the Pole, but keepeth ſtill in the ſame parallel: the like allowance is to be given to every quarter of the Compaſſe, as is layd downe upon this Northeaſt quarter.

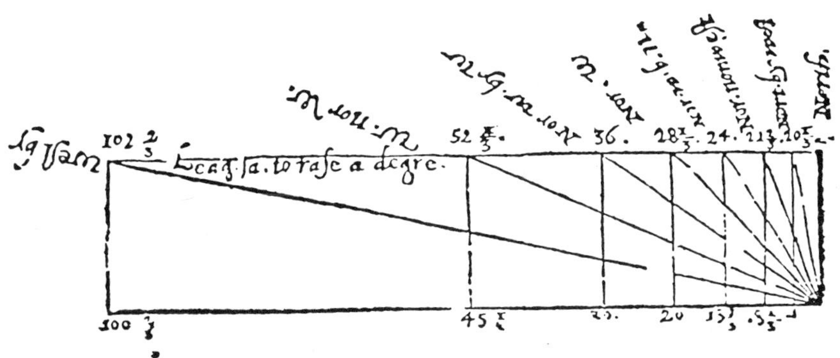

Leagues ſeparated from the Meridian in raiſing a degree.

Q. I perceive that degrees are to great purpoſe in Navigation. What is a degree?

Anſ. It is moſt true, that degrees are of very great imployment in Navigation, and a degree is the 360 part of a circle, how big or little ſoever the circle be, being applyed after ſixe seuerall sorts, for the better perfections of the practise Gubernautick, so that there be degrées of longitude, degrées of latitude, degrées of Azimuth, degrées of altitude, degrées applyed to measure, and degrées applyed to time.

A degree of longitude is the 360. part of the Equinoctiall.

A degree of latitude is the 360. part of the Meridian.

A degree of Azimuth is the 360. part of the Compasse or Horizon.

A degree of altitude is the 90. part of the verticall circle, or the 90. part of the distance betwéene the Zenith and the Horizon

Euery degree applyed to measure, doth containe 60. minutes, and euery minute 60. seconds, and euery second 60. thirds, &c. and euery degree of a great circle so applyed, containeth twentie leagues, which is 60. mile, so that euery minute standeth for a time in the account of measures, & a mile is limited to bee 1000. paces, euery pace 5. foote, euery foote 10. inches, and euery inch 3. barly cornes dry and round, after our English account, which for the vse of Nauigation is the onely best of all other: so by these rates of measure you may prooue that a degree is 20. leagues, or 60. miles, a minute is a mile or 5000. feete, a second is 83⅓. feete, and a third is 16⅔. inches: and thus much of degrees and their parts applyed to measure.

Of degrees applyed to time, there are 15. contained in euery houre, so that euery degree of time standeth in the account of time for 4. minutes, for an houre consisteth of 60 minutes of time, hath for his fifteenth part 4. minutes. so that a degrée being the fifteenth part of an houre, containeth 4 minutes of time, so that 15. degrées or 60 minutes make an houre, 24. houres make a naturall day, and 365. dayes 6. houres, are contained in a yeare: and thus much as touching time, and degrees applyed to time.

What is the vse of degrees?

THe vse of degrees is to measure distance betwéene place and place, to find altitudes, latitudes, and longitudes, to describe Countries, to distinguish courses, to finde the variation of the Compasse, to measure time, to finde the places and motions of all

all celestiall bodies, as the Sunne, Moone, Planets, and Starres to conclude, by degrées haue beene performed all Mathematicall obseruations whatsoeuer, whose vse is infinite.

What is the Poles altitude, and how it may be knowne?

Altitude is the distance, height, or mounting of one thing aboue another, so that the altitude of the pole, is the distance, height, or mounting of the Pole from the Horizon, and is defined to be that portion of the Meridian which is contained betweene the Pole and the Horizon, which altitude or eleuation is to bee found either by the Sunne, or by the fixed Starres, with the helpe of your Crosse staffe, Quadrant, or Astrolabie, but the Crosse staffe is the onely best instrument for the Seamans vse.

And in the obseruation of this altitude there are fiue things especially to be regarded: the first is, that you know your Meridionall distance betwéen your Zenith and the Sunne or Starres which by your Crosse staffe or Astrolabie is giuen: the second, that the declination bee truely knowne at the time of your obseruation. And the other thrée are, that you consider whether your Zenith be betwéene the Equinoctiall and the Sun or Starres, or whether the Equinoctiall be betwéene your Zenith and them, or whether they be betwéene your Zenith and the Equator, for there is a seuerall order of working vpon each of these thrée differences.

Latitude you must also know, that so much as the Pole is aboue the Horizon, so much is the Zenith from the Equinoctiall, and this distance betwéene the Zenith and the Equator is called latitude or widenesse, and is that portion of the Meridian which is included betwéene your Zenith and the Equator, for it is a generall rule for euer, that so much as the Pole is aboue the Horizon, so much the Zenith is from the Equinoctiall, so that in this sence, altitude and latitude is all one thing, the one hauing relation to that part of the Meridian, contained betwéene the Pole and the Horizon, and the other to that part of the Meridian which is contained betwéene the Zenith and the Equinoctiall.

You must further vnderstand, that betwéene the Zenith and Horizon, it is a quarter of a great circle containing 90. degrées, so that knowing how much the Sunne or any Starre is from the Horizon, if you take that distance from 90. the remainer is the distance betweene the said body and the Zenith. As for example, if the Sunne be 40. degrees 37. minuts from the Horizon, I substract 40. degr. 37. min. from 90. and there remaineth 49. deg 23. min. which is the distance betweene my Zenith and the Sunne &c. Those instruments that begin the account of their degrees at the Zenith, concluding 90. in the Horizon, are of most ease for the finding of the latitude by the Sunne or fixed Starres, because they giue the distance betweene the Zenith and the body obserued without further trouble. and that is the number which you must haue, and for which you doe search in your obseruation: all which things considered, you must in this sort proceed for the finding of the poles height or altitude.

By the Sunne or fixed Starres being between the Zenith and the Equinoctiall, the latitude is thus found, in what part of the world soever you be.

FIrst place the Crosse-staffe to your eye, in such good sort as that there may grow no errour by the disorderly vsing thereof, for vnlesse the Center of your staffe and the Center of your sight doe ioyne together in your obseruation, it will be erronious what you conclude thereby: your staffe so ordered then moue the transuersary vpon your staffe to and fro as occasion requireth, vntill at one and the same instant you may see by the vpper edge of your transuersary halfe the body of the Sunne or Starres, & that the lower edge or end thereof doe likewise touch the Horizon, at that place where it seemeth that the Skie and Seas are ioyned, hauing especiall regard in this your obseruation, as that you holde the transuersary as directly vpright as possible you may, and you must begin this obseruation somewhat before the Sunne or Starres be at South, and continue the same so long as you perceiue that they rise. for when they are at the highest, then are they vpon the Meridian, and then you haue the meridionall altitude which you seeke, at which time they will be due South from you, if your Compasse bee good and without variation, and then doth the transuersary shew vpon the staffe

the

the degrees and minutes that the said body is from your Zenith if the deg. of your Instrument be numbred from the Zenith to ward the Horizon: or else it sheweth the distance betweene the said body & the Horizon, if the deg. of your Instrument bee numbred from the Horizon, concluding 90. in the Zenith, as commonly Crosse staues are marked, which is not the easiest way: but if your staffe be accounted from the Horizon, then substract the degrees of your obseruation from 90 and the remainer sheweth the distance betweene your Zenith & the Sunne or Starres, which is ẏ number you must know: vnto that number so knowne by your Instrument, adde the declination of the body by which you doe obserue, whether it be the Sunne or any Starre, and that which commeth by the addition of those two numbers together, is the Poles height, or the latitude of the place where you are. as for example. In the yeare of our Lord 1621. the third day of March, the Sunne being then betweene my Zenith and the Equinoctiall, I obserued the Sunnes Meridionall altitude from the Horizon to be 72. deg. and 20 min. but because I must know the distance of the Sunne from my Zenith, I therefore substract 72. deg. 20. min. from 90. deg and there remaineth 17. deg 40. min. the distance of the Sunne from my Zenith, to that distance I adde the Suns declination for that day, which by my Regiment I finde to be 43. minuts 2. degrees of South declination, and it amounteth vnto 20. deg. 23. min. so much is the South pole aboue the Horizon, and so much is my Zenith South from the Equinoctiall, because the Sunne hauing South declination, and being betweene mee and the Equinoctiall, therefore of necessitie the Antartick pole must be aboue my Horizon.

89—60—the distance betweene the Zenith and the Horizon.	17–40–the suns di frō the Ze.
72—20—the Sunnes altitude.	2—43—Suns declination.
——— ———	——— ———
	20—23—Poles height.

When the Equinoctiall is betweene your Zenith and the Sunne or Starres, the altitude is thus found in all places.

By your Instrument as before is taught, you must seeke the Meridionall distance of the Sun or Starres from your Zenith,

nith, which being knowne, substract the declination of the Sun or Starres from the said distance, and the remaining number is the Poles height or latitude which you seeke: Example.

The 20. of October 1625. I finde by my Instrument that the Sunne is 60. deg. 45. min. from my Zenith at noone, being then upon the Meridian, the Equator being then betweene my Zenith and the Sunne, I also find by my Regiment that at that time the Sunne had 13. deg. 57. min. of South declination, because the Equinoctiall is betweene mee and the Sunne, therefore I substract the Sunnes declination from the obserued distance, and there resteth 46. deg. 48. min. the latitude desired, and because the Sunne hath South declination, and the Equinoctiall being betweene me and the Sunne, therefore I may conclude that the Pole Artick is 46. deg 48 min. aboue my Horizon, or that my Zenith is so much toward the North from the Equator.

g	m	
60	45	the Sunnes distance.
13	57	the declination.
46	48	the latitude.

When your Zenith is betweene the Sunne or Starres and the Equinoctiall, the Latitude is thus found.

By your Instrument as in the first example is shewed, you must obserue the Meridionall distance of the Sun or Stars from your Zenith, you must also by your Regiment or other Tables, search to know the declination of that body which you obserue, then substract the obserued distance from your Zenith out of the declination, and the remaining number is the latitude desired: Example. The Sunne hauing 20. deg. of North declination, and being upon the Meridian is 5 deg. 9. min. from my Zenith, I therefore substract 5. deg. 9. min. from 20. deg. and there resteth 14 deg. 51. min. the latitude desired: and because the Sunne hath North declination, my Zenith being betweene the Sunne and the Equinoctiall, therefore I conclude, that the North Pole is 14. deg. 51. min. aboue my Horizon.

the

g m
19—60—the declination.
5—9—the Sunnes distance from my Zenith.
— ——————
14—51—the Poles height

How shall I know the true order of placing the Crosse-staffe to mine eye, to auoyde errour in my obseruation?

TO finde the true placing of the staffe at your eye, thereby to amend the parallax or false shadow of your sight, doe thus: take a staffe hauing two crosses, a long crosse which endeth in 30. degrees, and a short crosse which beginneth at 30. deg. where the long crosse endeth, put the long crosse vpon his 30. deg. and there make him fast, then put the short crosse likewise vpon his 30. deg. there fasten him without mouing, then set the end of your staffe to your eye, mouing it from place to place about your eye, vntill at one instant you may see the endes of both crosses, which when you finde, remember that place and the standing of your body, for so must your staffe be placed, and your body ordered in all your obseruations.

Are these all the rules that appertaine to the finding of the Poles height.

Those that travell farre towards the North under whose Horizon the Sunne setteth not, shall sometime have occasion to seeke the latitude by the Sunne when the Sun is North from them, the pole being then betweene the Sunne and their zenith. When such observations are made, you must by your Instrument seeke the Suns height from the Horizon, substract that height from his declination, and the remaining number sheweth how farre the Equinoctiall is under the Horizon upon the poynt North, for so much is the opposite part of the Equator above the Horizon upon the poynt South, substract that Meridian latitude of the Equinoctiall from 90. and the remaining number is the Poles height desired: Example.

The Sunne having 22. degrees of North declination, his altitude from the Horizon is observed to be 3. degrees, 15. minuts, therefore substracting 3. deg. 15. min. from 22. degrees, there rest 18. deg. 45. min. which is the distance of the Equinoctiall from the Horizon, which being taken from 90. there resteth 71. deg. 15. min. the Poles elevation desired.

g m	g m
21-60-the Suns declinations	89-60-the dist betw. zen. & Ho.
3—15—the Suns altitude.	18-45-altitude of the Equator.
18—45—the altitude of the Equinoctiall.	71-15-the altitude of the pole.

But you must know that the declination found in your Regiment is not the declination which in this case you must use: for the Regiment sheweth the sunnes declination upon the Meridian or South poynt, in the place for whose Meridian the same was calculated, and not otherwise: therefore it is necessary to know the sunnes declination at all times, and upon every point of the Compasse: for I have beene constrained in my Northwest voyages, being within the frozen zone, to search the latitude by the sunne, at such time as I could see the sunne, upon what poynt of the Compasse soever, by reason of the great fogges and misties that those Northerne parts are subiect unto: and there is consideratiō also to be had upon euery difference of longitude for the Sunnes declination, as I haue by my experience found at my being in the Straights of Magilane, where I haue found the Sunnes declination to differ from my Regiment calculated for London, by so much as the Sunne declineth in fiue houres, for so much is the difference betweene the Meridian of London, and the Meridian of Cape Froward, being in the midst of the said Straights.

How may this declination be found for all times and vpon all poynts of the Compasse.

First consider whether the Sunne be comming towardes the Equinoctiall, or going from him, that being knowne, consider the time wherein you seeke the declination, then looke for the Sunnes declination in your Regiment for that day, and also seeke his declination for the next day, substract the lesser out of the greater, and the remainer is the whole declination which the Sunne declineth in 24. houres, or in his mouing through all the poynts of the Compasse, from which number you may by the rule of proportion finde his declination vpon euery poynt of the Compasse for euery houre of the day, as by these examples, may appeare: Example.

In the yeere 1625. the 20. of March, I desire to know the Sunnes declination when he is vpon the North part of the Meridian of London, I seeke the Sunnes declination for that day, and finde it to be 3. deg, 59. min. the Sunne then going from the Equator. I also search his declination for the next day, being the 21. of March, and finde it to be 4. deg. 22. min. I then substract 3. deg. 59. min from 4 deg 22. min and there resteth 23. min. so much the Sunne doth decline in 24. houres, or in going through all the poynts of the Compasse. Then I say by the rule of proportion, if 24. houres giue 23. minuts of declination, what will 12. houres giue &c. I multiply and diuide, and finde it to be 11. min. 30 sec. the Sunnes declination in 12. houres motion to bee added to the declination of the 20. day, being the Sunnes going from the Equator, or for the poynts of the Compasse, I may say,

If 32. poynts giue 22. min. of declination, what will 16. poynts giue, which is the distance betweene South and North? I multiply and diuide as the rule of proportion requireth, and find that 16. poynts giue 11. min. the Sunnes declination, in mouing through 16. poynts of the Compasse, which is to be added to the declination of the 20. day, because the Sunne goeth from the Equator, so I conclude the declination to be 3.d.52.min. the Sun being North the 20. of March.

In this worke the 30. seconds are omitted.

```
ho. mo.  ho.                |   po.  m.    po.   m.
24—23——12—11                |   32—22——16——11
   12                       |        16
  ______                    |       ____   3
   44    2                  |       132  3 5 2 (11
   22    2 6 4 (11          |       22   3 2 2
  ____   2 4 4              |       ____   3
   264   2                  |       352
```

Being West from the Meridian of London 90. degrees of longitude, I desire to know the Suns declination when the Sun is vpon the Meridian the 20. of March 1625. I must here consider that 90. deg. of longitude make 6. houres of time, for euery houre containeth 15. deg whereby I know that when the Sunne is South at London, he is but East from me, for when it is 12. of the clocke at London, it is but 6. of the clocke in the morning with me, and when it is 12. of the clocke with me, it is then 6. of the clocke in the afternoone at London: therefore I must seeke for the declination of the Sunne at 6. of the clocke in the afternoone, and that is the meridionall delination which I must vse being 90. deg. West from London which to doe, the last example doth sufficiently teach you, whereby you may easily gather the perfect notice of whatsoeuer is requisite in any of these kinde of obseruations, if you reade with the eye of reason, and labour to vnderstand with iudgement that which you read.

Example. The day and yeare proposed being the 20. of March 1625 declination the 3.d. 59. min the next day the 21 of March 4.d.22.min. Detraction made, resteth 23. min the proportionall part to be found for 90. deg. West, or 6. houres of time. Say if 24. houres giue 23. What 6 houres? Facit 5. min 18. seconds,

which

which being that the declination encreaseth, adde 5. min. 18. sec. to the declination for the day prefixed: that totall is the meridionall declination for 90. deg. of westerly longitude from the Meridian of London.

There is another way most excellent for the finding of the sunnes declination at all times, that is to search by the Ephemerides the sunnes true place in the Eclipticke for any time purposed whatsoever, and then by the Tables of Sinus the declination is thus knowne. Multiply the Sinus of the Sunnes longitude from the Equinoctiall poynts of Aries or Libra, to which soeuer he is neerest, by the Sinus of the sunnes greatest declination, and diuide the product by the whole Sinus, and the arke of the quotient is the declination desired: but because Seamen are not acquainted with such calculations, I therefore omit to speake further thereof, sith this plaine way before taught is sufficient for their purpose.

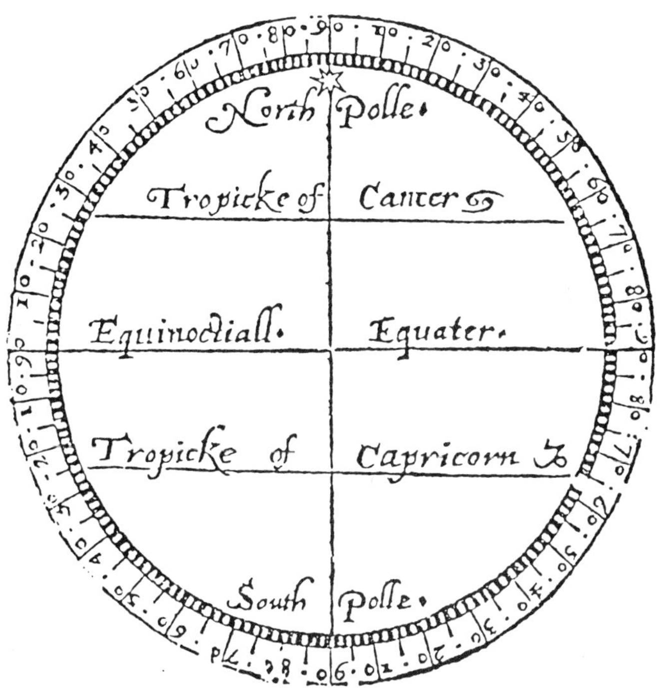

The vse of this Instrument.

By this instrument you may sufficiently vnderstand, the reasons of whatsoeuer is before spoken for the finding of the Poles eleuation, or the latitude of your being: into the consideration whereof because the yong practiser may the better enter, I thinke it not amisse by a few examples to expresse the necessary vse thereof.

1. Q. The Sunne being seauen degrees of North declination and the Pole Articke being 45. degrees aboue the Horizon, I demand what will be the Sunnes Meridionall distance from my Zenith?

1. A. First I turne the Horizon vntill I bring the North Pole to be 45. degrees aboue the same, there holding the Horizon not to be moued, I then bring the thrid that is fastened to the Center of the Instrument, 7 degrees from the Equinoctiall towardes the North, because the Sunne hath so much North declination, and the thrid doth shew me vpon the verticall circle, that the Sunne is 38 degrees from my zenith.

2. Q. The Pole Artick being 50. deg. aboue the Horizon, & the Sunnes distance 30. deg from the zenith, I demand what is the Sunnes declination?

2. A. As in the first question I place the North Pole 5. deg. aboue the Horizon, there holding the Horizon not to be moued, then I bring the thrid to the 30 degree vpon the verticall circle, because the Sunne is 30 degrees from my zenith, and then the thrid sheweth vpon the Meridian betweene the Tropick of Cancer and the Equinoctiall, that the Sunne hath 20 degrees of North declination.

3. Q. The Sunne hauing 10. deg. of South declination, being vpon the Meridian, is 53. deg. from my Zenith, I demand what is the Poles height?

3. A. In the first question the Poles height and the Sunnes declination are giuen for the finding of the Sunnes meridionall distance from the zenith. In the second the Poles height is giuen, & the Sunnes meridionall distance from the zenith, thereby to finde the Sunnes declination. And in this question the Suns declina-

declination and meridionall distance is giuen for the finding of the Poles height. I therefore bring the thrid fastned in the Center of the Instrument 10 degrées South from the Equator, betweene the Equinoctiall and the Tropicke of Capricorne, there holding the thrid not to be moued. I then turne to the Horizon untill I bring the 52 degree of the verticall circle under the thrid, and then the Horizon sheweth mee, that the North Pole is 43. degrees aboue the same.

4. Q. The Sunne hauing 12. degrées of South declination, and being upon the Meridian South from me, is 30. degrées aboue the Horizon, I demand how farre the Sunne is from my Zenith, how much the Equinoctiall is aboue the Horizon, and what is the Poles height?

4. A. First I bring the thrid to the place of the Sunnes declinatiō as before, there holding it not to be moued, then I turne the Horizon untill I bring it to be 30. deg. under the thrid, and then the thrid sheweth me that the Sunne is 60. deg. from my Zenith, and the Horizon sheweth that the Equinoctiall is 42. deg. aboue the same, and that the North Pole is also eleuated 48. deg. aboue the Horizon. Although these questions are so very easie and plaine, as that they may readily bee answered by memory, yet because the reasons how they are answered may the better appeare, is the cause wherefore they are demanded, and in this sort answered onely for the benefit of such as are not altogether expert in these practises, that thereby they might likewise frame unto themselues questions of other varietie, and so gather thereby the more sufficient iudgement in this part of Nauigation.

What is the Zenith?

The Zenith is that pricke or poynt in the heauens which is directly ouer your head, from whence a line falling perpendicularly, will touch the place of your being, & so passe by the Center of the Sphere, and this line may be called the Axis of the Horizon, and the Zenith the Pole of the same being 90. d. from all parts thereof, as by the former figure may most plainely appeare.

Forasmuch as the Poles height cannot be obſerved by the Sunne, vnleſſe the Sunnes true declination bee knowne, I haue therefore carefully calculated theſe Tables or Regiment, out of *Origanus*, for the yeare 1625. 6. 7. and 8. which will ſerue vntill the yeare 1644. without further correction: and becauſe there may grow no error by miſtaking the yeares, I haue ouer euery Moneth written the yeare of the Lord, in which the declination of the ſame Moneth is to be vſed, therefore when in any yeare and Moneth you ſeeke the Sunnes declination, firſt looke for the Moneth, and there you ſhall find 4. of thoſe Moneths, which are the Moneths between the leape yeares, then looke ouer each of thoſe moneths, vntill you find the yeare of the Lord, wherein you ſeeke the declination, and directly vnder that yeare is the Moneth wherein you muſt ſeeke the Suns declination: Example 1626. the tenth day of Feb. I would know the Suns declination, firſt I ſeeke out February, & vnder the ſecond yeare I ſee the yeare 1626. therefore this is my Moneth, againſt the tenth day of which Moneth I find that the Sun hath 10. deg. 49. min. of South declination, and after the like manner you muſt do in all the reſt as occaſion requireth.

Ianuary.

First.			Second.			Third.			Fourth.		
1625			1626			1627			1628		
1629			1630			1631			1632		
1633			1634			1635			1636		
1637			1638			1639			1640		
1641			1642			1643			1644		
D.	G.	M.	D.	G.	M.	D.	G.	M.	D.	G.	M.
1	21	47	1	21	49	1	21	51	1	21	54
2	21	37	2	21	39	2	21	42	2	21	44
3	21	27	3	21	29	3	21	31	3	21	34
4	21	16	4	21	18	4	21	21	4	21	24
5	21	5	5	21	7	5	21	10	5	21	13
6	20	52	6	20	56	6	20	59	6	21	2
7	20	41	7	20	44	7	20	47	7	20	50
8	20	29	8	20	32	8	20	35	8	20	38
9	20	17	9	20	19	9	20	22	9	20	25
10	20	4	10	20	6	10	20	9	10	20	12
11	19	50	11	19	59	11	19	56	11	19	59
12	19	37	12	19	35	12	19	42	12	19	46
13	19	21	13	19	20	13	19	28	13	19	32
14	19	1	14	19	5	14	19	14	14	19	18
15	18	52	15	18	50	15	18	59	15	19	3
16	18	37	16	18	34	16	18	44	16	18	48
17	18	21	17	18	25	17	18	28	17	18	33
18	18	5	18	18	9	18	18	13	18	18	17
19	17	49	19	17	53	19	17	57	19	18	1
20	17	32	20	17	36	20	17	40	20	17	44
21	17	15	21	17	19	21	17	33	21	17	28
22	16	58	22	17	2	22	17	6	22	17	11
23	16	41	23	16	45	23	16	49	23	16	53
24	16	23	24	16	27	24	16	31	24	16	36
25	16	5	25	16	9	25	16	13	25	16	18
26	15	47	26	15	51	26	15	55	26	16	0
27	15	28	27	15	32	27	15	36	27	15	42
28	15	9	28	15	13	28	15	18	28	15	23
29	14	50	29	14	55	29	14	59	29	15	4
30	14	31	30	14	35	30	14	40	30	14	45
31	14	11	31	14	16	31	14	20	31	14	25

South Declination. South Declination. South Declination.

February.

First.			Second.			Third.			Fourth.		
1625			1626			1627			1628		
1629			1630			1631			1632		
1633			1634			1635			1636		
1637			1638			1639			1640		
1641			1642			1643			1644		
D.	G.	M.	D.	G.	M.	D.	G.	M.	D.	G.	M.
1	13	51	1	13	56	1	14	0	1	14	15
2	13	31	2	13	36	2	13	40	2	13	55
3	13	9	3	13	15	3	13	20	3	13	35
4	12	50	4	12	55	4	13	0	4	13	14
5	12	29	5	12	34	5	12	39	5	12	54
6	12	8	6	12	14	6	12	19	6	12	33
7	11	48	7	11	53	7	11	58	7	12	12
8	11	26	8	11	31	8	11	36	8	11	50
9	11	5	9	11	10	9	11	15	9	11	29
10	10	43	10	10	49	10	10	54	10	11	7
11	10	21	11	10	27	11	10	32	11	10	45
12	10	0	12	10	5	12	10	10	12	10	23
13	9	36	13	9	43	13	9	48	13	10	1
14	9	15	14	9	21	14	9	26	14	9	39
15	8	53	15	8	58	15	9	4	15	9	16
16	8	30	16	8	36	16	8	42	16	8	53
17	8	8	17	8	14	17	8	19	17	8	31
18	7	45	18	7	51	18	7	56	18	8	8
19	7	22	19	7	28	19	7	33	19	7	45
20	6	59	20	7	5	20	7	10	20	7	2
21	6	36	21	6	42	21	6	47	21	6	58
22	6	13	22	6	19	22	6	24	22	6	35
23	5	50	23	5	56	23	6	1	23	6	12
24	5	27	24	5	32	24	5	38	24	5	48
25	5	3	25	5	9	25	5	15	25	5	24
26	4	40	26	4	46	26	4	51	26	5	0
27	4	16	27	4	22	27	4	28	27	4	37
28	3	53	28	3	58	28	4	4	28	4	13
									29	3	49

South Declination.

South Declination.

South Declination.

March.

First.				Second.				Third.				Fourth.		
1625				1626				1627				1628		
1629				1630				1631				1632		
1633				1634				1635				1636		
1637				1638				1639				1640		
1641				1642				1643				1644		
D.	G.	M.		D	G.	M.		D.	G.	M.		D.	G.	M.
1	3	29	South Declination.	1	3	35	South Declination.	1	3	41	South Declination.	1	3	23
2	3	6		2	3	11		2	3	17		2	3	0
3	2	43		3	2	48		3	2	53		3	2	35
4	2	19		4	2	24		4	2	30		4	2	11
5	1	55		5	2	0		5	2	6		5	1	49
6	1	31		6	1	37		6	1	42		6	1	25
7	1	7		7	1	13		7	1	19		7	1	1
8	0	43		8	0	49		8	0	55		8	0	38
9	0	20		9	0	26		9	0	31		9	0	14
10	0	4	Equi-	10	0	2	nocti-	10	0	8	all.	10	0	10
11	0	27		11	0	21		11	0	16		11	0	34
12	0	51		12	0	45		12	0	40		12	0	57
13	1	15		13	1	9		13	1	3		13	1	21
14	1	38	North Declination.	14	1	33	North Declination.	14	1	27	North Declination.	14	1	44
15	2	2		15	1	56		15	1	50		15	2	8
16	2	25		16	2	20		16	2	14		16	2	32
17	2	49		17	2	43		17	2	37		17	2	55
18	3	13		18	3	7		18	3	1[illegible]		18	3	19
19	3	36		19	3	30		19	3	25		19	3	41
20	3	59		20	3	53		20	3	48		20	4	5
21	4	22		21	4	15		21	4	11		21	4	28
22	4	43		22	4	39		22	4	34		22	4	51
23	5	[illegible]		23	5	3		23	4	57		23	5	14
24	5	31		24	5	26		24	5	[illegible]		24	5	37
25	5	54		25	5	49		25	5	43		25	6	0
26	6	17		26	6	12		26	6	6		26	6	23
27	6	39		27	6	34		27	6	29		27	6	45
28	7	2		28	6	56		28	6	51		28	7	9
29	7	25		29	7	19		29	7	4		29	7	30
30	7	47		30	7	41		30	7	36		30	7	52
31	8	9		31	8	4		31	7	58		31	8	15

F

Aprill.

First.			Second.			Third.			Fourth.		
1625 1629 1633 1637 1641			1626 1630 1634 1638 1642			1627 1631 1635 1639 1643			1628 1632 1636 1640 1644		
D.	G.	M.	D.	G.	M.	D.	G.	M.	D.	G.	M.
1	8	31	1	8	25	1	8	20	1	8	37
2	8	53	2	8	48	2	8	42	2	8	59
3	9	15	3	9	9	3	9	4	3	9	21
4	9	6	4	9	31	4	9	26	4	9	42
5	9	58	5	9	53	5	9	47	5	10	4
6	10	19	6	10	14	6	10	9	6	10	25
7	10	40	7	10	35	7	10	30	7	10	46
8	11	1	8	10	56	8	10	51	8	11	7
9	11	22	9	11	17	9	11	12	9	11	27
10	11	42	10	11	37	10	11	32	10	11	48
11	12	3	1	11	58	11	11	53	11	12	8
12	12	22	12	12	18	12	12	13	12	12	28
13	12	43	13	12	38	13	12	3	13	12	48
14	13	2	14	12	58	14	12	53	14	13	7
15	13	22	15	13	17	15	13	11	15	13	27
16	13	42	16	13	37	16	13	32	16	13	47
17	14	1	17	13	56	17	13	51	17	14	6
18	14	19	18	14	15	18	14	10	18	14	25
19	14	38	19	14	34	19	14	29	19	14	43
20	14	56	20	14	52	20	14	48	20	15	1
21	15	15	21	15	10	21	15	6	21	15	20
22	15	33	22	15	[illegible]	22	15	24	22	15	37
23	15	50	23	15	46	23	15	41	23	15	55
24	16	8	24	16	3	24	15	59	24	16	12
25	16	25	25	16	20	25	16	16	25	16	29
26	16	42	26	16	37	26	16	33	26	16	46
27	16	58	27	16	54	27	16	49	27	17	3
28	17	14	28	17	11	28	17	7	28	17	19
20	17	30	29	17	26	29	17	23	29	17	35
30	17	46	30	17	42	30	17	8	30	17	50

North Declination. North Declination. North Declination.

May.

First.			Second.			Third.			Fourth.		
1625			1626			1627			1628		
1629			1630			1631			1632		
1633			1634			1635			1636		
1637			1638			1639			1640		
1641			1642			1643			1644		
D.	G.	M.	D.	G.	M.	D.	G	M.	D.	G.	M.
1	18	2	1	17	58	1	17	54	1	18	6
2	18	17	2	18	13	2	18	10	2	18	21
3	18	32	3	18	28	3	18	24	3	18	36
4	18	46	4	18	43	4	18	39	4	18	50
5	19	0	5	18	57	5	18	54	5	19	4
6	19	14	6	19	11	6	19	8	6	19	18
7	19	28	7	19	25	7	19	21	7	19	32
8	19	41	8	19	38	8	19	35	8	19	45
9	19	54	9	19	51	9	19	48	9	19	57
10	20	7	10	20	3	10	20	0	10	20	10
11	20	19	11	20	16	11	20	13	11	20	22
12	20	31	12	20	28	12	20	25	12	20	34
13	20	42	13	20	39	13	20	37	13	20	45
14	20	53	14	20	51	14	20	48	14	20	56
15	21	4	15	21	2	15	20	59	15	21	7
16	21	15	16	21	12	16	21	10	16	21	18
17	21	25	17	21	22	17	21	20	17	21	28
18	21	35	18	21	30	18	21	3	18	21	37
19	21	44	19	21	42	19	21	40	19	21	46
20	21	53	20	21	51	20	21	49	20	21	55
21	22	2	21	22	0	21	21	58	21	22	4
22	22	10	22	22	8	22	22	6	22	22	12
23	22	18	23	22	16	23	22	1	23	22	20
24	22	25	24	22	23	24	22	12	24	22	27
25	22	32	25	22	51	25	22	29	25	22	34
26	22	39	26	22	37	26	22	36	26	22	41
27	22	45	27	22	44	27	22	42	27	22	47
28	22	51	28	22	50	28	22	48	28	22	53
29	22	57	29	22	56	29	22	54	29	22	58
30	23	2	30	23	1	30	22	59	30	23	3
31	23	7	31	23	6	31	23	4	31	23	8

North Declination.

North Declination.

North Declination.

Iune.

First.				Second.				Third.				Fourth.		
1625				1626				1627				1628		
1629				1630				1631				1632		
1633				1634				1635				1636		
1637				1638				1639				1640		
1641				1642				1643				1644		
D.	G.	M.		D.	G.	M.		D.	G.	M.		D.	G.	M.
1	23	11		1	23	10		1	23	9		1	23	12
2	23	15		2	23	14		2	23	13		2	23	16
3	23	18		3	23	17		3	23	17		3	23	19
4	23	21	North	4	23	21	North	4	23	20	North	4	23	22
5	23	24		5	23	23		5	23	23		5	23	25
6	23	26		6	23	26		6	23	25		6	23	27
7	23	28		7	23	18		7	23	27		7	23	29
8	23	30		8	23	29		8	23	29		8	23	30
9	23	31		9	23	30		9	23	30		9	23	30
10	23	31		10	23	31		10	23	31		10	23	31
11	23	31	Tro-	11	23	31	pi-	11	23	31	cks.	11	23	31
12	23	31		12	23	31		12	23	31		12	23	31
13	23	31		13	23	31		13	23	31		13	23	30
14	23	30		14	23	30		14	23	30		14	23	29
15	23	28		15	23	29		15	23	29		15	23	28
16	23	26		16	23	27		16	23	27		16	23	26
17	23	24		17	23	25		17	23	25		17	23	23
18	23	21	Declination.	18	23	22	Declination.	18	23	23	Declination.	18	23	21
19	23	18		19	23	19		19	23	20		19	23	17
20	23	15		20	23	16		20	23	17		20	23	14
21	23	12		21	23	12		21	23	13		21	23	10
22	23	7		22	23	8		22	23	9		22	23	5
23	23	2		23	23	3		23	23	4		23	23	0
24	22	57		24	22	58		24	22	59		24	22	55
25	22	51		25	22	53		25	22	54		25	22	50
26	22	45		26	22	47		26	22	48		26	22	44
27	22	39		27	22	41		27	22	42		27	22	37
28	22	32		28	22	34		28	22	36		28	22	31
29	22	25		29	22	27		29	22	29		29	22	23
30	22	18		30	22	20		30	22	22		30	22	16

Iuly.

First.			Second.			Third.			Fourth.		
1625			1626			1627			1628		
1629			1630			1631			1632		
1633			1634			1635			1636		
1637			1638			1639			1640		
1641			1642			1643			1644		
D.	G.	M.	D.	G.	M.	D.	G.	M.	D.	G.	M.
1	22	10	1	22	12	1	22	14	1	22	8
2	22	2	2	22	4	2	22	6	2	22	0
3	21	53	3	21	55	3	21	57	3	21	51
4	21	44	4	21	46	4	21	49	4	21	42
5	21	35	5	21	37	5	21	40	5	21	32
6	21	25	6	21	28	6	21	30	6	21	22
7	21	15	7	21	18	7	21	20	7	21	12
8	21	5	8	21	7	8	21	10	8	21	2
9	20	54	9	20	56	9	20	59	9	20	51
10	20	43	10	20	45	10	20	48	10	20	40
11	20	31	11	20	34	11	20	37	11	20	28
12	20	19	12	20	22	12	20	25	12	20	16
13	20	7	13	20	10	13	20	13	13	20	4
14	19	55	14	19	58	14	20	1	14	19	51
15	19	42	15	19	45	15	19	49	15	19	38
16	19	29	16	19	32	16	19	36	16	19	25
17	19	15	17	19	18	17	19	22	17	19	2
18	19	1	18	19	5	18	19	9	18	18	58
19	18	47	19	18	51	19	18	55	19	18	43
20	18	33	20	18	36	20	18	41	20	18	29
21	18	18	21	18	22	21	18	26	21	18	14
22	18	3	22	18	7	22	18	11	22	17	59
23	17	48	23	17	51	23	17	57	23	17	43
24	17	32	24	17	36	24	17	40	24	17	28
25	17	16	25	17	20	25	17	24	25	17	12
26	17	0	26	17	4	26	17	9	26	16	56
27	16	43	27	16	47	27	16	52	27	16	39
28	16	27	28	16	31	28	16	36	28	16	22
29	16	10	29	16	14	29	16	19	29	16	5
30	15	52	30	15	57	30	16	2	30	15	48
31	15	35	31	15	39	31	15	44	31	15	30

North Declination.

North Declination.

North Declination.

August.

First.			Second.			Third.			Fourth.		
1625			1626			1627			1628		
1629			1630			1631			1632		
1633			1634			1635			1636		
1637			1638			1639			1640		
1641			1642			1643			1644		
D.	G.	M.	D.	G.	M.	D.	G.	M.	D.	G.	M.
1	15	17	1	15	21	1	15	26	1	15	12
2	14	59	2	15	4	2	15	8	2	14	54
3	14	41	3	14	45	3	14	50	3	14	36
4	14	22	4	14	27	4	14	31	4	14	47
5	14	4	5	14	8	5	14	13	5	13	59
6	13	45	6	13	49	6	13	54	6	13	39
7	13	25	7	13	30	7	13	25	7	13	20
8	13	5	8	13	10	8	13	15	8	13	1
9	12	47	9	12	51	9	12	56	9	12	41
10	12	27	10	12	32	10	12	36	10	12	21
11	12	7	11	12	12	11	12	16	11	12	1
12	11	47	12	11	51	12	11	56	12	11	41
13	11	26	13	11	31	13	11	6	13	11	20
14	11	6	14	11	11	14	11	16	14	11	0
15	10	45	15	10	51	15	10	55	15	10	39
16	10	24	16	10	29	16	10	34	16	10	18
17	10	13	17	10	8	17	10	13	17	9	57
18	9	42	18	9	47	18	9	52	18	9	36
19	9	20	19	9	25	19	9	31	19	9	14
20	8	59	20	9	4	20	9	9	20	8	53
21	8	37	21	8	42	21	8	48	21	8	31
22	8	15	22	8	21	22	8	26	22	8	9
23	7	53	23	7	58	23	8	4	23	7	47
24	7	31	24	7	37	24	7	42	24	7	25
25	7	9	25	7	15	25	7	20	25	7	3
26	6	47	26	6	52	26	6	57	26	6	40
27	6	24	27	6	30	27	6	35	27	6	18
28	6	2	28	6	8	28	6	12	28	5	55
29	5	39	29	5	45	29	5	56	29	5	33
30	5	16	30	5	22	30	5	27	30	5	10
31	4	58	31	4	59	31	5	4	31	4	47

North Declination.

North Declination.

North Declination.

September.

First.	Second.	Third.	Fourth.
1625	1626	1627	1628
1629	1630	1631	1632
1633	1634	1635	1636
1637	1638	1639	1640
1641	1642	1643	1644

D.	G.	M.	D	G.	M.	D.	G.	M.	D.	G.	M.
1	4	36	1	4	36	1	4	41	1	4	24
2	4	18	2	4	13	2	4	19	2	4	1
3	3	44	3	3	50	3	3	55	3	3	38
4	3	21	4	3	27	4	3	32	4	3	15
5	2	54	5	3	4	5	3	9	5	2	52
6	2	35	6	2	40	6	2	46	6	2	28
7	2	17	7	2	17	7	2	23	7	2	5
8	1	44	8	1	54	8	1	59	8	1	41
9	1	35	9	1	31	9	1	36	9	1	18
10	1	7	10	1	7	10	1	13	10	0	55
11	0	33	11	0	43	11	0	49	11	0	31
12	0	14	12	0	20	12	0	26	12	0	35
13	0	10	13	0	4	13	0	2	13	0	16
14	0	33	14	0	27	14	0	22	14	0	40
15	0	56	15	0	51	15	0	45	15	1	3
16	1	20	16	1	14	16	1	9	16	1	27
17	1	43	17	1	38	17	1	32	17	1	50
18	2	7	18	2	1	18	1	56	18	2	14
19	2	31	19	2	25	19	2	19	19	2	37
20	2	54	20	2	48	20	2	43	20	3	0
21	3	17	21	3	11	21	3	6	21	3	24
22	3	41	22	3	35	22	3	30	22	3	47
23	4	4	23	3	58	23	3	53	23	4	11
24	4	28	24	4	22	24	4	16	24	4	34
25	4	51	25	4	45	25	4	40	25	4	57
26	5	14	26	5	8	26	5	3	26	5	20
27	5	37	27	5	32	27	5	26	27	5	44
28	6	0	28	5	55	28	5	49	28	6	7
29	6	23	29	6	18	29	6	12	29	6	29
30	6	46	30	6	41	30	6	35	30	6	22

North Declination. North Declination. North Declination.

Equi- nocti- all.

South Declination. South Declination. South Declination.

October.

First.			Second.			Third.			Fourth.		
1625			1626			1627			1628		
1629			1630			1631			1632		
1633			1634			1635			1636		
1637			1638			1639			1640		
1641			1642			1643			1644		
D.	G.	M.	D	G	M.	D.	G.	M.	D.	G.	M.
1	7	9	1	7	4	1	6	58	1	7	15
2	7	32	2	7	26	2	7	21	2	7	38
3	7	54	3	7	49	3	7	44	3	8	1
4	8	17	4	8	12	4	8	6	4	8	23
5	8	39	5	8	34	5	8	28	5	8	54
6	9	2	6	8	56	6	8	51	6	9	8
7	9	24	7	9	18	7	9	13	7	9	30
8	9	46	8	9	40	8	9	35	8	9	52
9	10	8	9	10	2	9	9	57	9	10	14
10	10	29	10	10	24	10	10	19	10	10	35
11	10	51	11	10	40	11	10	41	11	10	57
12	11	12	12	11	7	12	11	2	12	11	18
13	11	34	13	11	28	13	11	23	13	11	39
14	11	55	14	11	49	14	11	44	14	12	0
15	12	15	15	12	11	15	12	5	15	12	21
16	12	26	16	12	32	16	12	26	16	12	42
17	12	57	17	12	52	17	12	47	17	13	2
18	13	17	18	13	11	18	13	6	18	13	22
19	13	37	19	13	32	19	13	27	19	13	42
20	13	57	20	13	52	20	13	47	20	14	2
21	14	16	21	14	12	21	14	7	21	14	22
22	14	36	22	14	30	22	14	26	22	14	42
23	14	55	23	14	50	23	14	46	23	15	0
24	15	14	24	15	10	24	15	5	24	15	19
25	15	33	25	15	28	25	15	24	25	15	38
26	15	51	26	15	47	26	15	42	26	15	56
27	16	9	27	16	5	27	16	0	27	16	14
28	16	27	28	16	23	28	16	19	28	16	32
29	16	45	29	16	41	29	16	36	29	16	49
30	17	2	30	16	58	30	16	54	30	17	7
31	17	19	31	17	15	31	17	11	31	17	24

South Declination.

South Declination.

South Declination.

Nouember.

First.			Second.			Third.			Fourth.		
1625			1626			1627			1628		
1629			1630			1631			1632		
1633			1634			1635			1636		
1637			1638			1639			1640		
1641			1642			1643			1644		
D.	G.	M.	D.	G.	M.	D.	G.	M.	D.	G.	M.
1	17	30	1	17	32	1	17	28	1	17	40
2	17	52	2	17	48	2	17	44	2	17	57
3	18	8	3	18	5	3	18	1	3	18	13
4	18	24	4	18	20	4	18	17	4	18	28
5	18	40	5	18	36	5	18	32	5	18	44
6	18	55	6	18	51	6	18	47	6	15	59
7	19	10	7	19	6	7	19	2	7	19	13
8	19	24	8	19	21	8	19	17	8	19	28
9	19	38	9	19	35	9	19	31	9	19	42
10	19	52	10	19	48	10	19	45	10	19	55
11	20	5	11	20	2	11	19	59	11	20	9
12	20	18	11	20	15	12	20	12	12	20	22
13	20	31	13	20	28	13	20	25	13	20	34
14	20	43	14	20	40	14	20	37	14	20	46
15	20	55	15	20	52	5	20	49	15	20	58
16	21	6	16	21	4	16	21	1	16	21	9
17	21	17	17	21	15	17	21	12	17	21	20
18	21	28	18	21	26	18	21	23	18	21	31
9	21	38	19	21	36	19	21	33	19	21	41
20	21	48	20	21	46	20	21	43	20	21	51
21	21	58	21	21	56	21	21	53	21	22	0
22	22	7	22	22	4	22	22	2	22	22	9
23	22	15	2	22	13	23	22	11	23	22	17
24	22	23	24	22	21	24	22	19	24	22	25
25	22	31	25	22	29	25	22	27	25	22	33
26	22	38	26	22	36	20	22	35	26	22	40
27	22	45	27	22	43	27	22	42	27	22	47
28	22	51	28	22	50	28	22	48	28	22	53
29	22	57	29	23	56	29	22	54	29	22	59
30	23	3	30	23	1	30	23	0	30	23	4

South Declination.

South Declination.

South Declination.

December.

First.			Second.			Third.			Fourth.		
1625			1626			1627			1628		
1629			1630			1631			1632		
1633			1634			1635			1636		
1637			1638			1639			1640		
1641			1642			1643			1644		
D.	G	M.	D.	G	M.	D.	G.	M.	D.	G.	M.
1	23	8	1	23	6	1	23	5	1	23	9
2	23	12	2	23	11	2	23	10	2	23	13
3	23	16	3	23	15	3	23	14	3	23	17
4	23	20	4	23	19	4	23	18	4	23	21
5	23	23	5	23	22	5	23	21	5	23	24
6	23	25	6	23	25	6	23	24	6	23	26
7	23	28	7	23	27	7	23	27	7	23	28
8	23	29	8	23	29	8	23	29	8	23	30
9	23	30	9	23	30	9	23	30	9	23	31
10	23	31	10	23	31	10	23	31	10	23	31
11	23	31	11	23	31	11	23	31	11	23	31
12	23	31	12	23	31	12	23	31	12	23	31
13	23	30	13	23	31	13	23	31	13	23	30
14	23	29	14	23	30	14	23	30	14	23	29
15	23	28	15	23	28	15	23	29	15	23	27
16	23	26	16	23	26	16	23	27	16	23	25
17	23	23	17	23	24	17	23	24	17	23	22
18	23	20	18	23	21	18	23	22	18	23	19
19	23	17	19	23	17	19	23	18	19	23	15
20	23	13	20	23	14	20	23	14	20	23	11
21	23	8	21	23	9	21	23	10	21	23	7
22	23	3	22	23	4	22	23	6	22	23	2
23	22	58	23	22	59	23	23	0	23	22	56
24	22	52	24	22	53	24	22	55	24	22	50
25	22	46	25	22	47	25	22	49	25	22	43
26	22	39	26	22	40	26	22	42	26	22	37
27	22	32	27	22	33	27	22	35	27	22	30
28	22	24	28	22	26	28	22	28	28	22	22
29	22	16	29	22	18	29	22	20	29	22	14
30	22	7	30	22	9	30	22	12	30	22	5
31	21	58	31	22	1	31	22	3	31	22	56

South Tro- Declinatior. South picus. Declination. South Cancer. Declination.

What is the Chart?

THe Sea Chart is a speciall instrument for the Seamans vse, whereby the hydrographicall description of the Ocean Seas, with the answering geographicall limits of the earth, are supposed to be in such sort giuen, as that the longitudes and latitudes of all places, with the true distance and course betweene place and place, might be truely knowne. But because there is no proportionable agreement betweene a Globus superficies, and a plaine superficies, therefore a Chart doth not expresse that certaintie of the premisses which is thereby pretended to bee giuen, for things are best described vpon bodies agreeable to their owne forme. And whereas in the true nature of the Sphere, there can bee no parallels described but the East and West courses onely, the rest of the courses being concurred lines, ascendent toward the Poles, the Meridians all concurring and ioyning together in the Poles, notwithstanding in the Sea Chart all those courses are described as parallels, without any diuersitie, alteration or distinction to the contrary, whereby the instrument is apparantly faultie: yet it cannot be denyed but Charts for short courses are to very good purpose for the Pilots vse, and in long courses be the distance neuer so farre, if the Pilot returne by the same course, whereby in the first hee prosecuted his voyage, his Chart will be without errour, as an instrument of very great commoditie, but if he returne by any other way, then by that which he went forth, the imperfections of the Chart will then appeare to be very great, especially, if the voyage bee long, or that the same be in the North parts of the world, the farther towards the North, the more imperfect: therefore there is no instrument answerable to the Globe or paradoxall Chart, for all courses and climats whatsoeuer, by whom all declared truth is most plentifully manifested, as shall hereafter at large bee declared, but for the coasting of any shore or Country, or for short voyages, there is no instrument more conuenient for the Seamans vse, then the well described Sea-Chart.

What is the vse of the Sea Chart?

BY the directions of the Sea Chart the skilfull Pilot conueyeth his Shippe from place to place, by such courses as by the

Chart are made knowne unto him, together with the helpe of his Compasse or Crosse staffe as before is shewed, for the Crosse-staffe the Compasse, and the Chart, are so necessarily ioyned together, as that the one may not well be without the other in the execution of the practises of Nauigation: for as the Chart sheweth the courses so doth the Compasse direct the same, & the Crosse staffe by euery particular obserued latitude doth confirme the truth of such courses, and also giue the certaine distance that the Ship hath sayled upon the same.

And in the use or understanding of the Sea Chart, there are fiue things chiefly to be regarded.

The first is, that the Countries or geographie of the Chart be knowne, with euery Cape, Promontory, Port, Hauen, Bay, Sands, Rocks, and dangers therein contained.

Secondly, that the lines drawne upon the Chart, with their seuerall properties be likewise understood.

Thirdly, that the latitudes of such places as are within the Chart be also knowne, as by the Chart they are expressed.

Fourthly, that you be able to measure the distances betweene place and place upon the Chart.

And fiftly, the Seaman must bee able by his Chart to know the true courses betweene any Iles Continents, or Capes whatsoeuer, for by these fiue diuersities, the Chart is to be used in the skill of Nauigation.

How is the latitude of places knowne by the Chart?

The latitude is thus found by the Chart, upon the place whose latitude you desire to know, set one foote of your Compasses, then stretch the other foote to the next East & West line (for that line is your director) keeping that foote still upon the same line, moue your hand and Compasses East or West, as occasion requireth, untill you bring the Compasses to the graduated Meridian, and there that foote of the Compasses which stood upon the place whose latitude you would know, doth shew the latitude of the same place.

How is the course betweene place and place knowne?

WHen there are two places assigned, the course betweene which you desire to know, set one foote of your Compasses vpon one of the places, then by discretion consider the lines that lead toward the other place, stretching the other foote of the Compasses to one of those lines, and to that part of the line which is neerest to you, keeping that foote still vpon the same line, moue your hand and Compasses toward the other place, and see whether the other foote of the Compasses that stoode vpon the other place, doe by this direction touch the second place, which if it doe, then that line whereupon you kept the one foote of your Compasses, is the course betweene those places: but if it touch not the place, you must by discretion search vntill you finde a line, whereupon keeping the one foote of the Compasses, will lead the other foote directly from the one place to the other, for that is the course betweene those two places.

How is the distance of places found vpon the Chart?

IF the places be not farre a sunder, stretch a paire of Compasses betweene them, setting the one foote of the Compasses vpon one of the places, and the other vpon the other place, then not altering the Compasses, set them vpon the graduated Meridian of your Chart, and allowing 20. leagues for euery degree, that is contained betweene the two feete of your Compasses, the distance desired is thereby knowne: if betweene the places there be 5. degrees, then they are 100. leagues asunder, &c. But if the distance betweene the places bee so great, as that the Compasses cannot reach betweene them, then take out 5. degrees with your Compasses, which is 100. leagues, and therewith you may measure the distance as practise will teach you. There is also in euery Chart a scale of leagues laid downe, whereby you may measure distances, as is commonly vsed

How doth the Pilot order these matters, thereby to conduct his Ship from place to place.

THe Pilot in execution of this part of Nauigation, doth with carefull regard consider three especiall things, whereupon the full practises are grounded.

1. Of which the first is, the good obseruation of his latitude, which how it may be knowne is before sufficiently expressed.

2. The second is a carefull regard of his steredge, with very diligent examination of the truth of his Compasse, that it bee without variation or other impediments.

3. And the third is a carefull consideration of the number of leagues that the Ship sayleth in euery houre or watch, to the neerest estimation that possibly he can giue, for any two of these thrée practises being truely giuen, the third is thereby likewise knowne.

As by the Corse and height the distance is manifested, by the distance and Corse the height is knowne: by the height and distance the Corse is giuen, of which thrée things the Pilot hath onely his height in certaine: the Corse is somewhat doubtfull, and the distance is but barely supposed, notwithstanding from his altitude and Corse he concludeth the truth of his practise, procéeding in this sort.

First he considereth in what latitude the place standeth from whence he shapeth his Corse, which for an example shall bée the Lyzart standing in 50. degrées of septentrionall latitude, then directing his Corse S. W. sayleth 3. or 4. dayes or longer in such thick weather, as that hee is not able to make any obseruation of the Poles altitude, in which time hée omitteth not to kéepe an accompt how many leagues the ship hath sayled vpon that Corse as néere as he can gesse, which number of leagues in this example shall be 100. according to his iudgement: then hauing conuenient weather, he obserueth in what latitude he is, and findeth himselfe to be in 47. degrées, now with his Compasses he taketh the distance of 100. leagues, which is the quantitie of the Ships run by his supposition, and then setting one foote of the Compasses vpon the Lyzart, which is the place from whence he began his Corse, and directly S. W. from the same he setteth the other point of the Compasses, by the direction of another paire of Compasses, in such sort as Corses are found, and there he maketh a pricke for the place of his ships being, according to his reckoning and corse.

And now searching whether it doe agrée with his height, (for the height, corse, and distance must all agrée together) he findeth that his pricke standeth in 46. degrees 26. minutes but it should stand in 47. degrees to agree with his obseruation. Therefore perceiuing that he hath giuen the ship too much way, he bringeth his corse and obserued altitude to agrée, and then hee seeth that his ship hath sayled but 85. leagues, and there he layeth downe a pricke for the true place of his ships being, according to his corse and latitude, for so by his corse and height he findeth the truth of his distance, & reproueth his supposed accompt to be 15. leagues too much: and after this sort he proceedeth from place to place, vntill he arriue vnto his desired Port: which is a conclusion infallible, if there be no other impediments, (whereof there hath not beene good consideration had) which may breed errour, for from such negligence there may arise many inconueniences.

What may these impediments be?

By experience at the Sea we finde many impediments that so disturb the expected conclusion of our practice, as that they agrée not with the true positions of art. For, first it is a matter not common to haue the winde so beneficiall, as that a ship may sayle thereby, betwéene any two assigned places vpon the direct corse, but that by the contrarietie of winds, she may be constrained to trauers vpon all points of the Compasse, the nature whereof I haue before sufficiently expressed.

Secondly, although the wind may in some sort fauour, yet the ship may haue such a leeward condition, as that shee may make her way 2. or 3. points from her caping.

Thirdly, the steredge may be so disorderly handled, as that thereby the Pilot may be abused.

And lastly, the Compasse may be so varied, as that the Pilot may likewise thereby be drawne into errour, at all which things and many moe, as the nature of his sayling, whether before the wind, quartering or by a bowling, or whether with loftie or low sayles, with the benefits or hinderances of the Sea, tydegates, streames, and forced let thereof, &c. Of all which things (I say) the skilfull Pilot must haue carefull consideration, which are better learned by practise then taught by pen, for it is not possible that any man can be a good and sufficient Pilot or skilfull Seaman,

Seaman, but by painefull and diligent practise, with the assistance of art, whereby the famous Pilot may bee esteemed worthy of his profession, as a member méete for the Commonweale.

And now hauing sufficiently shewed you the ordering of your Chart, for the execution of the skill of Nauigation, and being also desirous that you should effectually vnderstand the full nature and vse of the same: I thinke it good by a few questions to giue you an occasion to exercise your selfe, in the perfect accomplishment of such conclusions as are by this excellent and commodious instrument to be performed.

Necessary questions for the better vnderstanding of the commodious vse of the Chart.

1. Q. If I sayle 70. leagues vpon the Southwest course. I demand how many degrées I shall lay or depresse the pole?

A. The difference will be 2. degrées, 30. minutes.

2. Q. If in sayling West Northwest I raise the pole 3. degrées, 30. minuts, I demand how many leagues I haue sayled?

A. The distance sayled, is 180 leagues.

3. Q. If in sayling 180. leagues betwéene West and North, I raise the pole 3. degrées, I demand vpon what corse I haue sayled, and how farre I am from the Meridian from whence I began that corse?

A. The corse sayled is N.w.b.w. and the distance from the Meridian is 90. leagues.

4. Q. If in sayling 154. leagues I be 80. leagues West from the Meridian from whence I began my corse, I demand vpon what point of the Compasse I haue sayled, and how much I haue raised the pole?

A. The corse is N. W. b. N. and the pole is raised 6. degrees.

5. Q. If I sayle N.w. vntill I be 50. leagues from the Meridian, where I began my corse; I demand how many leagues I haue sayled, and how much the pole is raised?

A. The distance sayled is 71. leagues, and the pole is raised 2. degrées, 32. minutes.

6. Q. If

6. Q. If in sayling W. N. W. I doe in 30. houres raise 2. degrées, how many degrées should I haue raised the pole, if the same motion had béene North and by West?

A. You should haue raised 5. degrées.

7. Q. A ship sayling towards the West, for euery 80. leagues that shee sayleth in her Corse, shee departeth from the Meridian from whence she began the same Corse 45. leagues, I demaund vpon what point of the Compasse, & how many leagues she hath sayled, in raising the pole 5. degrees?

A. She hath sayled Northwest by North 120. leagues.

8. Q. A Pylote sayling toward the West 100. leagues, hath forgotten his Corse, yet thus much he knoweth, that if he had sayled vpon such a corse, as that in 160. leagues sayling he would haue raised the pole 3. degrées, he should then haue beene twise as farre from the Meridian as now he is, and should also haue beene ½ degrées further to the Northward then now he is, I would now know what corse he hath sayled, how many leagues, and how farre he is separated from the Meridian from whence he began the said Corse.

A. Shée hath sayled 88. leagues Northwest by west, and is 73. leagues from the Meridian néerest.

9. Q. Two shippes departing from one place, the one sayling 145. leagues towards the West, hath raised the pole 4. degrees, and the other hath raised the pole 7. degrees, and is 95. leagues West from the Meridian of the place from whence he began his Corse, I demand by what corse the said ship hath sayled, how farre they be asunder, and by what corse they may meete?

A. The first ship hath sayled Northwest by west, the second hath sayled Northwest by north 170. leagues, they are asunder 65. leagues, and the Corse betwéene them is North northeast, and South southwest.

10. Q. Two ships sayling from one place, the one in sayling 180. leagues, is to the Eastward of the Meridian where he began his corse 150. leagues, I demand vpon what corse and how many leagues the other ship shall sayle, to bring himselfe 50. leagues N. by W. from the first ship?

A. The first ship hath sayled N. e. by e. and hath raised the pole 5. degrées, the second ship must sayle Northeast by north 237. leagues.

Lthough it may ſeeme (to ſome that are very expert in Nauigation) that theſe queſtions are needleſſe, and without vſe, being ſo plaine as not deſeruing in this ſort to be publiſhed, notwithſtanding that their opinion, I doe in friendly curteſie aduiſe all young practiſers of this excellent Art of Sayling, that they doe not onely by their Charts prooue the truth of theſe anſwered queſtions, but alſo endeuour themſelues to propound diuers other ſorts of queſtions, and in ſeeking their anſweres to enter into the reaſon thereof: for by ſuch exerciſe, the yong beginner ſhall vnderſtand the ſubſtantiall grounds of his Chart, and grow perfect therein: for whoſe eaſe and furtherance onely, I haue at this preſent publiſhed this briefe treatiſe of Nauigation, knowing that the expert Pylot is not vnfurniſhed of theſe principles, but every little helpe doth greatly further in euery beginning: and therefore for the further benefit of the practiſer, I haue hereunto annexed a particular Sea Chart of our Channell, commonly called the Sleue, by which all that is before ſpoken as touching the vſe of the Chart, may be practiſed, wherein the depths of the Channell are truely layd downe: being an inſtrument moſt commodious and neceſſary for all ſuch as ſeeke the Channell cõming out of the Ocean Sea, much of it is from my own practiſe, the reſt from Pylots of very good ſufficiency: I haue found great certaintie by the vſe of this Chart, for by the altitude and depth I haue not at no time miſſed the true notice of my Ships being, which (through Gods merciful favour) by my lands falls I haue found alwaies to be without terrour, therefore haue it not in light regard, for it will giue you great euidence, and is

worthy

worthy to be kept as a ſpeciall iewell for the Seamans vſe, be he neuer ſo expert.

And thus hauing ſufficiently expreſſed all the practiſes appertaining to the skill of Horizontall Nauigation, which kinde of ſayling is now of the greateſt ſort onely practiſed, I thinke it good for your better memory briefly to report that which before is ſpoken as touching this kinde of Nauigation, and withall it will not be amiſſe to ſhew you after what ſort I haue beene accuſtomed to keepe my accompts in my practiſes of ſayling, which you ſhall finde to be very ſure, plaine, and eaſie, whereby you may at all times examine what is paſt, and ſo reforme the cauſes layd downe vpon the Chart, if by chance there ſhould any errour be committed. And ſo concluding his part of Nauigation, will in the next treatiſe make knowne vnto you the vſe of the Globe, ſuch vſes I meane as the Seaman may practiſe in his voyages, and that are moſt neceſſary for his knowledge.

A Table shewing the order how the Seaman may keepe his accompts, whereby hee may at all times distinctly examine his former practises, for in euery 24. houres, which is from noone to noone, hee doth not onely lay downe his latitude, with the corse and leagues, but also how the winde hath blowne in the same time.

The first Columne is the moneths and dayes of the same, the second is the obserued altitude, the third is the Horizontall corse or motion of the Ship, the fourth the number of leagues that the Ship hath sayled, the fifth is a space wherein must be noted, by what winde those things haue beene performed: and the next great space is to lay downe any briefe discourse for your memory.

Moneths and dayes of the moneth.	Latitude. G	M.	Anno. 1593. Corse.	Leages	Winde.	The 23. of March, cape S Augustine in Brasill being sixteen leags East from me, I began this accōpt.
March. 24	7	30	N.N.E	25	East	
25	5	44	N.b.E.nor.	36	E.b.N.	Compasse varied 9. d. the South point west-
26	4	1	N.b.N.	35	E.b.N.	ward
27	2	49	N.	24	E.b.N.	Compasse varied 8 d. the South point west-
28	1	31	N. esterly.	26	E.b.N.	ward.
29	1	4	N.N.W.	9	N.E.	Compasse varied 6. d.
Aprill. 31	0	0	N.b.W.	21	E.N.E.	40 m. the South point westward.
4	0	39	N.W.b.N.	15	N.E.	Obseruation, the Pole artick aboue the Hori-
7	1	53	N.N.W.	28	N.E.	zon.
9	3	5	N.W.b.N.	30	N.e.b.e.	
10	4	5	N.W.b.N.	22.	N.e.	
11	4	45	N.W.	18	N.e.b.N.	
12	5	16	N.W.	14	N.e.b.N.	
13	6	11	N.W.b.N.	23	N.e.	Compasse varied 7. d. the North point east-
14	7	16	N.W.b.N	24	N.e.	wards.

A briefe repetition of that which is before spoken.

There are thrée kindes of Nauigation, Horizontall, Paradoxall, and sayling vpon a great Circle, performed by Corse and Trauers.

A Corse is the paradoxall line, which is described by the ships motion vpon any point of the Compasse.

A Trauers is the varietie of the ships motion vpon euery alteration of Corses.

The Compasse is an artificiall Horizon, by which Corses and Trauerses are directed, and containeth 12. points, and euery point containeth 11 $\frac{1}{4}$. degrées, or 45. minutes, being $\frac{1}{4}$ of an houre.

By such quantitie of time as the Moone separateth her selfe from the Sunne, by the like rate of time euery tide doth one differ from another.

In euery houre the tyde altereth two minutes, in euery floud twelue minutes, and in euery ebbe twelue minutes, and in euery day 48. minutes, because that so is the Moones separation from the Sunne: for the Moone doth separate her selfe from the Sunne, in euery day one point and 3. minutes, betwéene the change and the full shée is to the Eastwards of the Sunne, and then is her separation, at which time shée is before the Sunne in respect of her naturall motion, but in regard of her violent motion, shée is then behinde or abaft the Sunne.

Betwéene the full and change, shée is to the westward of the Sunne, applying towards the Sunne, and then is her application, at which time shée is behinde or abaft the Sunne, in respect of her naturall motion, but in consideration of her violent motion, shée is then before the Sunne.

Shée hath a violent motion, a naturall motion, a slow swift and meane motion.

In euery 27. dayes and 8. houres, shée performeth her naturall motion through the Zodiac.

Betwéene change and change there is twentie nine dayes twelue houres, fortie foure minutes néerest.

The solar yéere consisteth of 12. moneths, and the lunar yéere of 12. Moones.

The Moones age is found by the Epact.

All instruments vsed in Nauigation, of what shape or forme soeuer they be, are described or demonstrated vpon a Circle, or some portion of a Circle, and therefore are of the nature of a Circle.

A degrée is the 360. part of a Circle, how bigge or little soeuer the Circle be.

A degrée is applyed after the 6. seuerall sorts, to the Equator, to the Meridian, to the Horizon, to the verticall Circle, to measure to time.

Altitude is the distance, height, or mounting of one thing aboue another.

The Poles altitude is the distance betweene the Pole and the Horizon, or the portion of the Meridian which is contained betweene the Pole and the Horizon.

The altitude of the Sunne aboue the Horizon, is that portion of the verticall circle, which is contained betweene the Horizon and the Sunne.

Latitude, is that arke of the Meridian which is contained betweene the parallell of any place and the Equator, or that part of the Meridian which is included betweene the Zenith and the Equinoctiall.

Longitude, is that portion of the Equator contained betweene the Meridian of S. Mihels, one of the Iles of the Assores, and the Meridian of the place whose longitude is desired: the reason why the accompt of longitude doth begin at this Ile, is because that there the Compasse hath no varietie, for the Meridian of this Ile passeth by the poles of the world, and the poles of the Magnet, being a Meridian proper to both poles.

The longitude betweene place and place, is the portien of the Equator, which is contained betweene the Meridian of the same places.

Declination is the distance of the Sunne, Moone, & Starres, from the Equinoctiall, or that part of the Meridian which passeth by the Center of any celestiall body, and is contained betweene the same center and the Equinoctiall.

Hidrography is the description of the Ocean Sea, with all Iles, bancks, rocks, and sands therein contained, whose limits extend

extend to the geographicall borders of the earth, the perfect notice whereof is the chiefest thing required in a sufficient pylot, in his excellent practise of Sayling.

Geography is the description of the earth onely, whereby the terrestriall forme in his due situation is giuen, whose distinction is by mountaines, riuers, vallies, cities, & places of fame, without regard of Circles, Climats, and Zones.

Cosmography is the description of the heauens, with all that is contained within the circuite thereof, but to the purpose of Nauigation, we must vnderstand Cosmography to be the vniuersall description of the terrestriall Globe, distinguished by all such circles, by which the distinction of the celestiall Sphere is vnderstood to be giuen, with euery Country, Coast, Sea Harborow, or other place seated in their due longitude, latitude, zone, and Clyme.

The Chart is a speciall instrument in Nauigation, pretending the Cosmographicall description of the terrestriall Globe, by all such lines, circles, corses, and diuisions as are required to the most exquisite skill of Nauigation.

The end of the First Booke.

THE SECOND PART OF THIS TREATISE OF NAVIGATION.

WHEREIN IS TAVGHT the nature and most necessary vse of the Globe, with the Circles, Zones, Climates, and other distinctions, to the perfect vse of SAYLING.

By which most excellent Instrument is performed all that is needfully required to the full perfection of all the three kindes of Nauigation.

zenith
Meridian
Cancer
Northe

THE SECOND BOOKE OF THE *SEAMANS SECRETS*

What is the Sphere?

The Sphere is a solide body contayned vnder one superficies, in the middest whereof there is a poynt or prick, which is the center of the Sphere, from whence all right lines drawne to the circumference, are equall the one to the other, whereby it is to bee vnderstood, that the center of the Sphere is euenly placed in his midst, as that it hath like distance from all parts of the Circumference. And for as much as the Sphere is an Instrument demonstrating vnto vs the vniuersall ingine of the world, wée must therefore vnderstand this center to be this terrestriall Globe wherein we haue our being, which compared to the Celestiall Globe or heauenly Circumference doth here proportion, as the Center to his circle: which earthly globe by the diuine mighty workmanship of God, doth admirably hang vpon his Center, being of equall distance from all parts of the Circumference.

What are the distinctions of the Sphere?

The Sphere is distinguished by the ten circles, whereof 6 are great circles, and 4. are lesse circles: whereof there are only 8, described vpon the body of the globe, limiting the zones and motion of the Planets, as the Equinoctiall, the Ecliptick, the Equinoctial Colure, the Solstitial Colure, the Tropick of Cancer, the Tropick of Capricorne, the Articke Polar Circle, & the

 Antarc-

Antartick Polar Circle. The Horizon and Meridian are not described upon the body of the globe, but artificially annexed thereunto for the better perfection of his use.

Which are the great Circles, and which the lesser?

The Equator, the Ecliptick, the 2. Colures, the Meridian and the Horizen, ere great circles, because they divide the sphere into 2. equall parts. The 2. Tropickes, the Polar circles, are lesser circles, because the devide the Sphere into two unequall parts.

Which is the Equator or Equinoctiall?

The Equinoctiall is a great circle devlding the Sphere into two equall parts, leauing the one halfe towards the North, and the other halfe towards the South, and is equally distant from both the Poles of the world 90. degrees, placed euenly betwéene them, and described upon them, this line crosseth the Horizon in the true poynts of East and West, and hath alwayes the one halfe aboue the Horizon, unlesse it bée under either of the Poles, for there the Equator is in the Horizon: it crosseth the Meridian at right Sphericke angles, and it also crosseth the Ecliptick line in the first minute of Aries and Libra, deuiding the Ecliptick and Horizen, and is also by them deuided into two equall parts. This line is also deuided into 360. equall parts or degrées, which are the degrees of Longitude, beginning the account in the poynt of Aries, reckoning towards the East, concluding the number 360. in the place where the first account began viz. where the Equator doth intersecte the Ecliptick in the first minute of Aries, under which Meridian S. Mihels one of the yles of the Assores to be placed in the geographicall description of the terrestriall Globe.

What is the vse of the Equator?

The use of the Equinoctiall, is to know the declination of the Sunne, Moone, and Starres, whereby the latitude of places is giuen, for that portion of the Meridian which is contayned betweene the Equator and the Center of the Sunne,, Moone, or Starres, is their declination: also by the Equinoctiall is knowne the

the Longitude of places, for a quarter of a great Circle being drawne from the Pole, to the place whose Longitude is desired, and so continued to the Equinoctiall, that degree and minute in which the quarter Circle doth touch the Equator, is the Longitude of the same place, or if you bring any place (that is described upon the Globe) whose Longitude you would know, under the Meridian of the Globe, that degree of the Equinoctiall that is then likewise directed under the Meridian, is the Longitude desired: When the Sunne commeth upon the Equator, then the dayes and nights are of one length throughout the whole world, and then the Sunne riseth upon the true poynt of East, and setteth upon the true poynt of West, and not els at any time. This circle being fixed in the firmament is moued with the first mouer in euery houre 15. degrees, by which accompt in 24 houres his motion is performed. And here note, that the degrées of the Equinoctiall haue a double application, the one to time, and the other to measure: in respect of time 15. degrees make an houre, so that euery degree contayneth but 4. minuts of time, but when his degrees haue relation to measure, then euery degree contayneth 60. minuts, being 20. leagues, of that euery minute standeth for a mile after our English accompt.

But this allowance of 20. leagues to euery degree of the Equinoctiall, in sayling, or measuring of distances upon the East & West Corses, is onely when you are under the same, because the Equinoctiall being a parallell, is likewise a great circle, and euery degrée of a great circle is truely accompted for 20. leagues or 60. miles.

But in the rest of the parallells where either of the Poles are eleuated aboue the Horizon, if there you sayle or measure upon the Corses of east or west, there are not 20. leagues to be allowed to euery degrée, because such parallells are lesser Circles, therefore they haue the fewer number of leagues to euery degrée: so that the further you depart from the Equator, the lesser are the parallells, and the lesser that any parallell is, the lesser are his degrées, because euery circle contayneth 360. degrées, and as the circles and degrées are diminished in their quantity, in like sort the distance answerable to such degrées, must abate, as their circles doe decrease. And further know, that the Equator is the be-

beginning of all terrestriall Latitude, and declination of the celestiall bodies.

What is the Eclipticke?

THe Ecliptick line is a great circle, deuiding the Sphere into two equall parts, by crossing the Equator in oblique sort deuiding him, & being deuided by him into two equall parts, bending from the Equator towardes the North and South 23. degrées, and 28. minutes, being in the first minute of Cancer and Capricorne, there determining the Tropicall limits, this line likewise deuideth the Zodiac, by longitude into 2. equall parts, and is deuided together with the Zodiac, into 12. equall portions called signes, and euery of these signes is deuided vpon the Ecliptick into 30. equall parts or degrees, so that this line is deuided into 360. degrées, vpon which line the center of the Sun doth continually moue: this circle is described vpon his proper poles, namely the Pole of the Zodiac, being in all his parts 90. degrées from either of them.

The Zodiac is a circle contrary to all the other, for they are Mathematicall lines, consisting onely of length, without breadth or thicknesse: but the zodiac hath latitude or breadth 12. degrees, whose limits are 6. degrees of either side of the Ecliptick, wherin the Sunne, Moone and Planets performe their motions and reuolutions, the center of the Sunne onely kéeping vpon the Ecliptick, but the other Planets haue sometime North latitude, and sometime South latitude. And here you must vnderstand, that the latitude of the Planets or Starres, is that portion of the Eclipticall Meridian which is contained betwéen the center of the Planet or Starre, and the Ecliptick line, and their longitude is that portion of the line Ecliptick, which is contained betwéene the sayd Meridian and the Eclipticall Meridian that passeth by the poles of the Zodiac, and the first minute of Aries.

The 12. diuisions or signes of the Zodiac, are these, Aries ♈, Taurus ♉, Gemini, ♊, Cancer ♓, Leo ♌, Virgo ♍, Libra ♎, Scorpio ♏, Sagittari ♐, Capricorne ♑, Aquarius ♒, Pisces ♋: and these are their Characters that stand by them.

The 7. Planets that keepe within the limit of the Zodiac, are these: Saturne ♄, Iupiter ♃, Mars ♂, Sol ☉, Venus ♀, Mercury ☿, Luna ☽, Saturne performes his course through all the degrees of

the

the Zodiac, once in euery 30. yeares: Iupiter in 12. yeares: Mars in 2. yeeres, the Sunne in 365. dayes and 6. houres being one yeare, Venus and ☿, as the Sunne, and the Moone perfor-meth her course in 29 dayes and about 8. houres, through all the degrees of the Zodiac.

And note that this naturall motion of the Planets in the Zo-diac, is from the West toward the East, the diurnall motion is violent, caused by the first mouer, or primum mobile, who in e-uery 24. houres doth performe his circular motion from the east to the west, carrying with him all other inferiour bodyes what-soeuer.

What is the vse of the Zodiac.

By the Zodiac and Ecliptick is knowne the Longitude and Latitude of any Celestiall body, either Planets or fixed Starres, for a quarter of a great circle drawne from the pole of the Zodiac to the center of any Planet or Starre, and so conti-nued vntill it touch the Ecliptick, that degree and minute where the sayd quarter-circle toucheth the Ecliptick, is the longitude of the sayd body, which is to be accompted from the first minute of Aries, for the longitude of Aries is the portion of the Ecliptick which is contayned betweene the ecliptical meridian pas-sing by the poles of the Zodiac, and the first minute of Aries, and the ecliptical meridian which passeth by the poles of the Zo-diac and the center of any planet or starre.

When the Planets are vpon the Northside of the Ecliptick, they haue North latitude, and being South from the Ecliptick, they haue South latitude.

Also the motions of the Planets, the time of any Eclipse, and the Sunnes declination by his place in the Ecliptick, are knowen by this Circle, whose vse is very ample and to great purpose for all Astronomicall considerations.

What are the Colures?

The Solstitiall Colure is a great circle passing by the poles of the world, and the poles of the Zodiac and the Solstitiall poynts or first minute of ♑, and ♋, cutting the Equinoctiall at right Spherick angles, in his 90. and in his 270. degrees.

The

The Equinoctiall Colure is likewise a great circle passing by the poles of the world, and the equinoctiall poynt of ♈, and ♎, and crosseth the equator in his first & 18. degrees, and these Colures do intersect each other in the poles of the world to the right Sphericke angles.

What is the vse of these Colures?

Their vse is to distinguish the foure principall seasons of the yeare, Spring, Summer, Autumne, and Winter, deuiding the Equator and Ecliptick into 4. equall parts: also that Arke of the Solsticiall Colure which is included betweene the first minute of ♋, and the Equinoctiall, is the Sunnes greatest declination toward the North, the like Arke being betweene the tropicall poynt of ♑, and the Equator, is the Sunnes greatest South declination, being in these our dayes 23 degrees, 28. minutes.

What is the Tropick of Cancer?

The Tropick of ♋, is one of the lesser Circles deuiding the Sphere into two vnequall parts, and is described vpon the pole Artick, a parallell to the Equator, 23. degrees, 28. minutes from him, being the farthest limit of the Ecliptick bending towards the North, to which when the Sunne commeth, the dayes are then longest to all those that inhabite the North parts of the world, and shortest to the southerne inhabitants: betweene this circle & the equator are concluded the 6. septentrional signes, ♈, ♉, ♊, ♋, ♌, ♍, in which signes during the time that the Sun abideth, being from the 11. of March, to the 13. of September, he hath North declination, and then is the spring and summer to all such as inhabite in the North parts of the world: and Autumne and Winter to the Inhabitants of the south parts of the world: this circle doth touch the Ecliptick in the first minute of ♋, where the Sunne beginneth his returne toward the South, whereupon it tooke the name Tropick, which signifieth conuersion or return, by which poynt of the Ecliptick, the diurnall motion describeth this circle.

What is the Tropick of Capricorne?

THe Tropick of ♑, is one of the lesser Circles deuiding the Sphere into two vnequall parts, and is described vpon the pole Antartick a parallell to the Equinoctiall 23 degrees, 28 minutes from him being the farthest bending of the Ecliptick towards the South, to which when the Sunne commeth, the daies are then longest to all those that inhabite in the South parts of the world and shortest to the Northern Inhabitants: betweene this circle and the Equator are included the 6 Southern signes, ♎, ♏, ♐, ♑, ♒, ♓, in which signes during the time that the Sun abideth, being from the 13. of September to the 11. of March, he hath South declination, and then is the spring and the Summer to all such as inhabite the South parts of the world: and Autumne and Winter to all the inhabitants in the North parts of the world: this circle toucheth the Ecliptick in the first minute of ♑, by which point the diurnall motion describeth this parallell.

What is the vse of the The Tropicks?

BY the Tropicks the Sunnes declination is knowne, as also the tropickes by the Sunnes farthest motion towardes the North and South, for so much as the Tropicks are distant from the Equator, so much is the Sunnes greatest declination: and such as is the Sunnes greatest declining, such is the distance betweene the Tropicks & the Equator: they are also the limits of the burning zone, separating the burning and temperat zones. For betweene the two Tropicks, is contained the burning zone.

What is the Artick polar Circle?

THe artick Polar Circle is one of the lesser Circles, diuiding the sphere into two vnequall parts, and described vpon the Pole Articke in parallell, to the Tropick of ♋, hauing such distance from the pole as the Tropick hath from the Equator, being 23. degrees, 28. minutes, vpon which circle the Artick pole of the Zodiac is placed, which being fixed in the firmament, by the vertue of the first mouer is carried about with the heauens, by which motion this circle is described.

What is the Antartick polar circle?

The Antarticke polar circle is opposit to the Artick, and parallell to the Tropick of ♑, being in all respect of such distance and description, from and about the pole Antartick, as the Artick polar circle is about the pole Artick.

What is the vse of Artick and Antartick polar circles?

The vse of these two polar Circles, is to shew the distance of the poles of the Zodiac, from the poles of the World, for so much as the Solsticiall points are distant from the Equator, so much are the poles of the Zodiac from the poles of the World: the Circles doe also diuide and limit the temperate and frozen zones for betweene the Tropicke of ♋ and the Artick polar Circle is contained the Northern temperate zone, and betwéene the Artick polar Circle & the pole Artick, that is within the Artick polar circle is contained the Northern frozen zone. Also between the Tropick of ♑, and the Antartick polar Circle, is contained the Southern temperate zone, and within the said polar Circle, is included the Antartick frozen zone, and these are all the Circles that are described vpon the body of the Globe.

What is the Meridian?

The Meridian is a great Circle passing by the poles of the World, and by your Zenith, diuiding the horizon into two epuall parts, in the points North and South, it also diuideth the Sphere with all the parallell Circles therein contained, into 2. equall parts, crossing them at right Spherick angles. And this Meridian is not fixed in the firmament as the rest of the Circles are, for if it were, then should it be moued with the first mooner as the rest are, but it is not so: therefore the Meridian is manifested vpon the Globe by a circle or ring of copper fastned vnto the Globe, vpon the 2. poles, so that the Globe moueth round vpon his 2. poles within the Meridian: this Meridian is graduated in euery of his quarters into 90. degrees, by which his vse is performed: and note that one Meridian may haue many Horizons, yet euery Horizon hath but one Meridian, for if you trauaile

uaile South or North, you keepe still vpon the same Meridian, yet in euery sensible difference of distance you shall enter into a change of horizons, for there be as many Horizons as there be sensible differences of distance and there be as many Meridians as there be sensible differences of distance, so that the difference be not vpon the poynts North and South, but this copper Meridian annexed to the Globe is to be applyed to all differences and distances whatsoeuer, as amply as if the number were infinite.

What is the vse of the Meridian?

The vse of the Meridian is to know the highest ascending of the Sunne, Moone or Starres from the horizon, for when they be vpon the Meridian, then are they farthest from the Horizon, and then is the most conuenient time to take the altitude of the Sunne or Starres, whereby to finde the poles eleuation.

By the Meridian of your Globe is knowne the latitude and longitude of any place vpon the Globe contained, for if you bring any place vnder the Meridian, the degrees of the Meridian doe shew the latitude of the same, and that degree of the Equator which the Meridian doth crosse is the longitude &c.

What is rhe Horizon?

The Horizon is a great circle diuiding the heauens into two equall parts, the one halfe being aboue the horizon is alwayes in sight, the other halfe is not seene being vnder the Horizon, and therefore is called the finitor or limit of our sight, for where the heauens and seas seeme to ioyne together, that is the Horizon: the Horizon is not fixed in the firmament, and yet is a fixed circle constant to his proper latitude, but because in the Globe one and the same Horizon may performe whatsoeuer is required to all eleuations, the Horizon is so artificially annexed to the Globe, that by the motion of the Meridian, in the same there faulteth nothing in his vse: and the Horizons in all respects distinguished, as in the Sea Compasse. There are two kindes of Horizons, a right Horizon, and an oblique Horizon: when the Poles are in the Horizon, then it is a right Horizon, for then the Equa-

Equator doth cut the Horizon to right angles, making a right Sphere and a right Horizon, an oblique horizon is where eyther of the Poles are eleuated aboue the same, for then the equator doth cut the Horizon to vnlike angles, making an oblique Sphere, and an oblique Horizon, and although the horizons be diuers and many in number, for euery sensible difference of distance hath his proper Horizon, yet is the horizon of the Globe so conueniently annexed thereunto, as that by the mouing of the Meridian in the horizon, and by the Globes motion in the Meridian, both the Horizon and Meridian are to be applyed as proper to all places whatsoeuer, and note that the place where you are, is alwayes the center of the plaine superficiall horizon.

What is the vse of the Horizon?

The Horizon is the beginning of all altitude, for whatsoeuer is aboue the horizon, is sayd to haue altitude more or lesse, and by the horizon such altitudes are giuen with helpe of the Crosse staffe, for placing the Crosse staffe at your eye, if by the one end of the transuersary you see the horizon, and by the other end (at the same instant) you see the body obserued, then doth the transuersary shew vpon the staffe the altitude desired, by the horizon the nauigable courses from place to place are likewise knowne, as also the quantitie of the rising and setting of the Sunne, Moone, and starres: whereby is knowne the length of the dayes and nights in all climates and at all seasons: by the horizon is knowne vpon what degree of Azumuth the Sunne, Moone, or Starres are, when they may be seene, in what part of the heauen soeuer, whereby the variation of the Compasse is found, and the Poles altitude may at all seasons be giuen.

Are these all the circles appertaining to the Globe?

There are other circles which are fixed and doe properly appertaine to euery particular horizon, as Azumuths, Almicanters, the Articke, and Antarticke Circles.

What are circles of Azumuth?

Circles of Azumuths, or verticall circles, are quarters of great circles, concurring together in the Zenith, as the Meridians plane doe in the pole, and are extended from the Zenith to every degree of the horizon, &c. And because they cannot be conveniently described upon the Globe to be applyed to all horizons, therefore upon the Meridian of the Globe there is a peice of copper artificially placed, to be remoued to any degree of the Meridian at pleasure, which piece of copper representeth the Zenith, and must alway be placed so many degrees from the Equator, as the pole is eleuated from the horizon, and unto this Zenith there is ioyned a quarter of a great Circle called Quarta altitudo, the ende whereof doth continually touch the horizon, and is so ioyned to the Zenith, as that it may be mooued round upon the horizon, and to every part thereof at your pleasure: this Quarta altitudo is deuided into 90 degrees, being the distinction of all altitude, and beginneth the account from the horizon, which is the beginning of altitude, and concludeth 90. degrees in the Zenith, being the end and extreame limit of all altitude.

What are Almicanters?

Almicanters or Circles of altitude, are parallell circles to the horizon, & are described upon the Zenith, as the parallels to the Equator, are described upon the Poles, of which circles there are 90 answerable to the distinctions of the Quarta altitudo, which are the degrees contained betweene the horizon and Zenith, these circles cannot be described upon the Globe, to be applyed to every horizon, but they are distinguished by the circular motion of the Quarta altitudo, for if I desire to see the Almicanter circle of 10. degrees, by mooving the Quarta altitudo round about the horizon, the Zenith degree of their quarter circle, doth shew the Almicanter desired, in what eleuation soever.

What is the vse of these two circles?

The Quarta altitudo performeth the use of both, by the Quarta altitudo and horizon the courses from place to place are knowne, according to the true horizontall position, as hereafter shall plainly appeare: it also sheweth the degree of Azumuth, and obserued altitude of any celestiall body, in what latitudes soever: by the Quarta altitudo and horizon, you may describe a paradoxall Compasse vpon the Globe, the Poles height is at all times thereby to be knowne, and the variation of the Compasse is thereby likewise giuen, as hereafter in the practise you shall be taught.

What are the Artick and Antartick circles?

Euery horizon hath his proper Artick or Antartick circle, those horizons that haue the pole Artick eleuated aboue them, haue their proper Artick circle, and those that haue the South pole eleuated, haue their proper Antartick circle, the quantitie of which circle is according to the Poles eleuation, for if the pole be much eleuated, then is the Artick circle great, for the poles altitude is the semidiameter of this circle, if the pole be in the Zenith, then halfe the heauens is the Artick circle.

What is the vse of this circle?

If the Sunne, Moone or any Starres be within this Circle, they are neuer carried vnder the horizon during the time of their abode therein, whereupon it commeth to passe, that such as trauaile far towardes the North, haue the Sunne in continuall view, and those that inhabite vnder the pole (if any so doe) the Sunne is in continuall sight for sixe moneths together, because the sixe Septentrionall signes are within the Artick circle, the Equator being in the horizon &c.

There is another small circle, which is called Circulus horarius, or the houre circle, to be annexed to the Meridian of the Globe, for the perfection of his vse, this circle must be diuided into 24. equall parts or houres, and those againe into such parts as you please for the better distinction of time: this circle must be fastned to the Meridian, so that the houres 12 must stand directly vpon the edge of the Meridian, and the Pole must be the center of this circle, vpon which pole there must be fastened an Index to moue proportionably as the Sphere (vpon any occasion) shall be moued.

There is also an halfe circle, called the Circle of position, which sith it serueth to no great purpose for Nauigation, I here omit, and thus is the Globe fully finished for the perfection of this vse.

What are the Poles of the world?

There are two Poles, the North articke Pole, and the South or Antartick Pole, which poles are two immoueable prickes fixed in the firmament, whereupon the Sphere is moued by vertue of the first mouer, and are the limits of the Axis of the world, as also the extreame terme or band of all declination, being 90. degrees from all parts of the Equator.

By the raysing of the Pole from the horizon, is knowne the parallell or latitude of our being, it also giueth the quantitie of the Artick circle, and obliquitie of the Sphere.

What is the Axis of the world?

The Axis of the world is a right line passing by the center of the Sphere, and limited in the Circumference, about the which the Sphere moueth and is therefore called the Axis of the, Sphere and as all lines commensurable are limited betweene two poynts or prickes, so is the Axis of the world, and those two limiting prickes are called the Poles of the world.

What are the Poles of the Zodiac?

The Zodiac hath likewise two Poles, Articke and Antarticke, being two prickes fixed in the firmament, limiting the Axis of the Zodiac, and are distant from the poles of the world 23. degrees 28. minutes, which poles by the motion of the sphere do describe the Poles circles, performing their motion about the poles of the world in euery 24. houres, by vertue of the first mouer, pon these poles the Ecliptick, and Zodiac is described: also a quarter of a great circle garduated into 90. degrees, being fastened to eyther of these Poles and brought to the center of the Starre, sheweth by that graduation the latitude of the same Starre, and where the quarter circle toucheth the Ecliptick that is likewise his longitude, also the 7. Planets doe performe their naturall reuolutions vpon these poles, whose motion is from the West towardes the East, contrary to the motion of the first mouer.

What is the Axis of the Zodiac?

The Axis of the Zodiac, is a right line passing by the center of the Sphere, and limited in the circumference, whose limiting poynts are the poles of the Zodiac, and his Axis is mooued by the Sphere as are his Poles.

What are the Poles of the Horizon?

There are two Poles of the horizon, which are the limits of his perpendicular dimetient, being equidistant 90. degrees from

from all parts of the horizon, and are the extreame limits of all altitude, that pole which is in the upper hemisphere is called the Zenith, and his opposite Pole is called Nadir, they are extended in the firmament, but not fixed in it, for they moue neuer, but remaine alwayes stable to their proper horizon, which could not be if it were fixed in the firmament, for then should they be moued with the firmament as the rest are, by the helpe of these Poles is found the Azimuth and Almicanter of any celestiall body, for a quarter circle deuided into 90. degrees, and fixed to the Zenith, as is the Quarta altitudo, being mooued to any celestiall body, doth by those degrees shew the almicanter or altitude of the same body from the horizon, and that part of the horizon which the quarter circle teacheth, is the azimuth of the same body, alwaies prouided that the Zenith stand answerable to the poles eleuation, that is, so many degrees from the Equator, as the Pole is from the Horizon.

How many Zones be there?

There are 5 Zones, two temperate zones, two frozen zones, and one burning zone, the burning zone lieth betwéene two Tropickes, whose latitude is 46. degrées, 56. minutes, which zone by ancient Geographers is reported to be not habitable, by reason of the great heate which there they supposed to be, through the perpendicularitie of the Suns beames, whose perpetuall motion is within the sayd zone, but we finde in our trauels, contrary to their report, that it is not onely habitable, but very populous, containing many famous and mighty nations, and yéeldeth in great plenty the most purest things that by natures benefits the earth may procreate: twice I haue sayled through the zone, which I found in no sort to be offensiue, but rather comfortable vnto nature, the extremitie of whose heate is not furious but tolerable, whose greatest force lasteth but 6. houres, that is from 9. of the clocke in the morning, vnto 3. in the afternoone, the rest of the day and night is most pleasing and delightfull: therefore they did nature wrong in their rash report.

Of the frozen Zones.

The frozen Zones are contained within the polar circle, the Articke frozen zone within the Artick polar circle, and the Antarticke frozen zone within the Antartick polar circle, which are also reported not to be habitable, by reason of the great extremitie of colde, supposed to be in those parts, because of the Sunnes farre distance from those Zones, but in these our dayes wée finde by experience, that the ancient Geographers had not the due consideration of the nature of these zones, for thrée times I haue béene within the Artick frozen zone, where I haue found the ayre very temperate, yea and many times in calme weather maruellous hot: I haue felt the Sunnes beames of as forcible action within the frozen zone in calmes néere vnto the shore, as I haue at any time found within the burning zone: this zone is also inhabited with people of good stature, shape, and tractable

 con-

conditions, with whom I haue conuersed, and not found them rudely barbarous, as I haue found the Caniballes which are in the straights of Magilane, and Southerne parts of America: In the frozen zone I discouered a coast which I named Desolation at the first view thereof, supposing it by the loathsome shape to bee wast & desolate, but when I came to anchor within the harbours thereof, the people presently came vnto me without feare, offering such poore things as they had to exchange for yron nayles, and such like: but the Caniballes of America flie the presence of men, shewing themselues in nothing to differ from bruit beasts: thus by experience it is most manifest that those zones which haue béene estéemed desolate and wast, are habitable, inhabited and fruitfull. If any man be perswaded to the contrary of this truth, he shall doe himselfe wrong in hauing so base an imagination of the excellency of Gods creation, as to thinke that God creating the world for mans vse, and the same being deuided but into 5. parts, thrée of those parts should be to no purpose: but let this saying therefore of the Prophet Esay be your full satisfaction, to confirme that which by experience I haue truly spoken: *For thus sayth the Lord that created heauen, God himselfe that framed the earth and made it, he that prepared it, he created it not in vaine, he framed it to be inhabited, &c.* Esay 45. 18.

Of the temperate Zones.

The temperate Artick zone is included betwéene the Tropick of ♋ and the Artick polar circle, whose latitude or breadth is 42. degrées, 2. minutes, within the which we haue our habitation.

The temperate Antartick zone is limited by the Tropick of ♑, and the Antartick polar circle, and hath breadth or latitude 42. degree. 2. minutes.

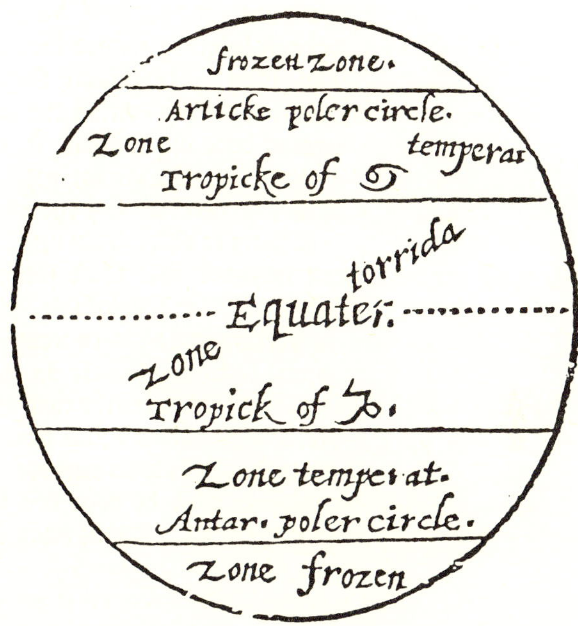

What is a Climate?

A Climate is the space or difference upon the upper face of the earth, included betwéen two parallels, wherein the day is sensibly lengthened or shortened halfe an houre, for as you travaile from the Equater toward the Artick Pole, the Sunne having North declination, the dayes doe grow longer and longer untill at last the Sunne not setting under the Horizon, you shall have continuall day, and every space or distance that altereth the day halfe an houre, is called a Climate these: Climates take their names from such famous places as are within the said Climates, of which there are nine, as by their distinctions may appeare.

1. The first passing through Meroe, beginneth in the latitude of 12. deg. 45. m. and endeth in 20. d. 30. m. whose breadth is 7. d. 45. m.

2. The second passing through Syene, beginneth in the latitude of 20. deg. 30. m. and endeth in 27. d. 30. m. whose breadth is 7. d.

3. The third passing through Alexandria, beginneth in the latitude of 27. d. 30. m. and endeth in 33. d. 40. m. whose breadth is 6. d. 10. m.

4. The fourth passing by Rhodes, beginneth in the latitude of 33. deg. 40. m. and endeth in 35. deg. whose breadth is 5. deg. 20. m.

5. The fifth passing by Rome, beginneth in the latitude of 39. deg. and endeth in 43. deg. 30. m. whose breadth is 3. deg. 45. m.

6. The sixt passing by Boristhines, beginneth in 43. deg. 39 min. and endeth in 47. deg. 15. min. whose breadth is 3. deg. 45. m.

7. The seuenth passing by the Riphæan mountaines, beginneth in 47. d. 15. m. and endeth in 50. d. 20. m. whose breadth is 3. d. 5. m.

8. The eight passing by Mæotis or London, beginneth in 50. deg. 20. m. and endeth in 52. deg. 10. m. whose breadth is 2. d. 50. m.

9. The ninth passing by Denmarke, taketh his beginning in the latitude of 53. d. 10. m and endeth in the latitude of 35. d. 30. m. and hath in breadth 2. d. 20. m.

If you desire to know how many leagues euery Climate is in breadth, allow for euery degrée 20. leagues, or 60. miles, and for euery minute a myle, so is the distance giuen.

Thus haue I manifested vnto you all the diuisions and particularities of the Spheres distinction.

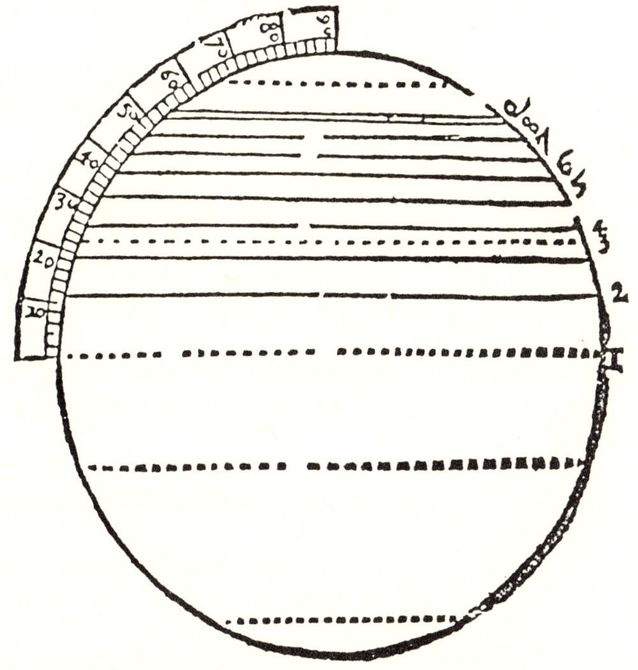

What is the vse of the Globe?

The vse of the Globe is of so great ease, certaintie, and pleasure, as that the commendations thereof cannot sufficiently be expressed, for of all Instruments it is the most rare and excellent, whose conclusions are infallible, giuing the true line, angle and circular motion of any Corse or Trauers that may in Nauigation happen, whereby the longitude and latitude is most precisely knowne and the certaintie of distance very plainly manifested according to the true nature thereof: it giueth the variation of the Compasse, and the houre or time of the day at all seasons, and in all places. And by the Globe the poles height may at all instants and vpon euery poynt or Azimuth of the Horizon by the Sunnes altitude taken be most precisely knowne, by the certaintie of whose excellent vse, the skilfull Pilot shall receiue great content in his pleasing practise gubernautick.

How are distances measured upon the Globe?

VVhen there are two places assigned, the distance betwéene which you desire to know, with a payre of circular Compasses you must do it in this sort: set one foote of the Compasses upon one of the places, and the other foote upon the other place, the Compasses so stretched forth, bring unto the Equator and as many degrées as may be contained betwéene these two poynts of the Compasse, allowing 20. leagues for every degrée is the distance desired: or if the places be of such distance as that you cannot with your Compasses reach them, then take with your Compasses 5. degrées of the Equator, which is 100. leagues, or 10. degrées, for 200. leagues, and so measure how often the distance is contained betwéene the said places, if any part of a degrée doth remain, for halfe a degrée allow 10 leagues, for a quarter 5. leagues, &c. But if you desire a most exquisite precisenesse in measuring to the minute, second and third, then doe thus. When your Compasses doth fall upon any part of a degrée, note the distance betwéene the end of that degrée and the poynt of the Compasses, then with a paire of convenient Compasses take the distance, then measure the same 60 times upon the Equator, (beginning at some certaine place) then consider how many degrées are contained within the measure, and allow every degrée to be a minute or mile, so are the leagues and miles knowne, if any part of a degrée remaine upon this measure of minuts, doe as at the first, measuring the same 60. times upon the Equator, the degrées comprehended within the measure, are seconds: if any parcell of a degrée remaine upon these seconds, do as in the first, and the degrées contained in this measure are thirds, and so you may procéede infinitely.

How may the Globe be rectified answerable to the true position of the heavens, for any place, or promontory.

The place being knowne for which you would rectifie the Globe, doe thus: bring the place under the Meridian, & there consider the latitude thereof: and as many degrées as that place is from the Equator, so many degrees you must elevate the pole from the Horizon, then bring the Zenith directly over the sam

place

place, and so is your Globe rectified for the execution of any practise: and without this ordering of the Globe, there is no conclusion to be executed by the same.

How is the longitude of places knowne by the Globe?

By turning the Globe within the Meridian, you must bring the Promontory Bay, Harborow, Citie, or other place (whose latitude and longitude you seeke) precisely under the Meridian, there holding the Globe steady, the degree of the Meridian that is directly over the said place, sheweth the latitude thereof, and that degree of the Equinoctiall which is directly under the Meridian is the longitude of the same place.

How is the Corse found betweene place and place?

Two places being assigned, the Corse betweene which you desire to know, first seeke the latitude of one of these places, and rectifie the Globe answerable unto the same, as before is taught, then bring that place directly under the Meridian and Zenith, if both places be under your Meridian, they then lie North and South, if not then bring the Quarta altitudo to the other place, and note upon what part of the Horizon the end of the same toucheth, for that is the precise Horizontall Corse betweene the said places, but this you must consider, that the Horizontall Corse is not the nauigable Corse, unlesse the places be of small distance, for if any place beare Northeast from me, or East from me, or upon any other poynt, North or South excepted, and be distant 500. leagues, if I sayle upon the Horizontall Corse, I shall neuer arriue unto the same place.

How then shall the Pilote sayle by the Globe, if the matter be so doubtfull?

The skilfull Pilote that useth this excellent instrument, doth first consider the place from whence he shapeth his Corse, and rectifieth the Globe answerable to the same, then bringing the

the place directly vnder the Meridian and Zenith, there holding the Globe steadie, bringeth the Quarta altitudo to the place for which he is bound, the end whereof sheweth vpon the Horizon the true Horizontall Corse, vpon which Corse hee sayleth 20. or 30. leagues, and there maketh a note or pricke by the edge of his Quarta altitudo, according to the true distance proued by Corse, reckoning an altitude as in the vse of a Chart: then he bringeth that pricke or note vnder the Meridian, and there considereth the true latitude of his being, he then rectifieth the Globe answerable to the same pricke, and keeping the same vnder the Zenith. doth againe turne to the Quarta altitudo to the place for which hee is bound, the end whereof sheweth vpon the Horizon the Horizontall Corse, then sayling as at the first, he maketh a note or pricke as before, and thus prosecuting his Corse, shall arriue vnto his desired place: but in this practise hee shall plainely proue that his Horizontall Corse will differ greatly and that by his sayling in this sort he shall by his notes and prickes describe the true nauigable and neerest Corses betweene the said places: The like methode is to be obserued vpon any trauers or forced course whatsoeuer: and therefore the Pilote must take care, that although the wind be neuer so fauourable, yet he must not prosecute any Horizontall Corse (North and South onely excepted.)

Therefore I say the Pilote must take speciall care to consider the distance of places, whether the Horizontall Corse will lead him betweene the said places, for if places be more then 45. degrees asunder, the Horizontall Corse is not the meane to finde those places, vnlesse they lie North and South: for the Horizontall course betweene any two places, is a portion of a great circle, which being of large distance, must be performed by great circle Nauigation, and not by Horizontall Corses for the collection of many Horizontall Corses being knit together, doe performe a paradoxall motion, altogether differing from a great circle: as for an example: being at Cape verde, there is a place distant from mee 80. degrees, vpon the poynt Northwest, vnto which place I desire to sayle, I therefore bring Cape verde vnder the Meridian of my Globe, there considering the latitude of the Cape, I raise the Pole answerable to the same, and place the Zenith directly ouer the Cape, then turning the Quarta altitudo to the point Northwest vpon the Horizon all such places as the said Quarta altitudo then toucheth, doe beare due Northwest from me now prosecuting this Corse by the direction of my Compasse, the first day I sayle 20. leagues, therefore I make a marke by the edge of the Quarta altitudo, 20. leagues from the Zenith, then bringing that mark vnder the Meridian, I rectifie the globe answerable to the latitude thereof, the next day I sayle other 20. leagues vpon the same poynt, and make a marke as at the first, I bring that marke likewise vnder the Meridian, and rectifie the Globe as before, and by this methode prosecuting the Corse N. W. I shall describe a paradoxall line, which will lead mee to the North of the place vnto which I would sayle, the farther the distance, the greater the difference: by this order you may describe paradoxall lines, vpon all the poynts of the Compasse, but this is to be regarded, that your differences be as small as you may, and that none of them exceede 20. leagues, for by the smallest distinctions, is performed the greatest certaintie. And by the description of these lines, you may very manifestly vnderstand the difference of Horizontall paradoxall and great circle Nauigation.

And this may suffice for the sayling vse of the Globe, conuenient for the Seamans purpose.

What is the great Circle Nauigation?

Great Circle Nauigation is the chiefest of all the 3. kindes of sayling, in whom all the other are contained & by them this kinde of sayling is performed, continuing a Corse by the shortest distance betweene places, not limited to any one Corse, eyther horizontall or paradoxall, but by it these Corses are ordered to the full perfection of this rare practise. whose benefits in long voyages are to great purpose. ordering and disposing all horizontall trauerses to a perfect conclusion: for there are many changes of horizontall and paradoxall Corses in the execution of this practise, so that vpon the shifting of a winde, when that it may seeme that you are forced to an inconuenient Corse by the skill of great Circle sayling, that Corse shall be found the shortest and onely proper motion to performe your voyage. And also when with fauourable windes the Pilote shall shape a Corse by his Chart or Compasse paradoxall, as the best meane to attaine his Port, he shall by this kinde of sayling find a better and shorter Corse, and by sufficient demonstration proue the same, so that without this knowledge I see not how Corses may be ordered to their best aduantage: therefore sith by it the perfection of sayling is largely vnderstood, and the error likewise most substantially controled, it may of right chalenge the chiefest place among the practises Guberrautick. The particularities whereof if I should by an orderly methode labour to expresse, it would be a discourse ouer-large for this place, and as I thinke troublesome if the premises be not well vnderstood: therefore I will now ouer-passe it, vntill a time more conuenient and of better leasure.

Of paradoxall Nauigation.

Paradoxall nauigation, demonstrateth the true motion of the Ship vpon any Corse assigned, in his true nature by longitude, latitude, and distance, giuing the full limit or determination of the same, by which motion lines are described neither circular nor straight, but concurred or winding lines, and are therefore called paradoxall, because it is beyond opinion that such lines should be described by plaine horizontall motion: for the full perfection of which practise I purpose (if God permit) to publish a paradoxall Chart, with all conuenient speede and so will discouer by the same at large, all the practises of paradoxall and great circle nauigation, for vpon the paradoxall Chart, it will best serue the Seamans purpose, being an instrument portable, of easie stowage and small practise, performing the practises of Nauigation as largely and as beneficially as the Globe in all respects: and all these practises of sayling before mentioned, may in a generall name be aptly called Nauigation Geometricall, because it wholly consisteth of Geometricall demonstratiue conclusions

But there is another knowledge of Nauigation, which so farre excelleth all that is before spoken, or that hath hitherto bin vulgarly practised, as the substance his shadow, or as the light surpasseth the thicke obscured darknesse: and this sweete skill of

sayling

sayling may well be called Navigation Arithmeticall, because it wholly consisteth of Calculations, comprehended within the limit of numbers, distinguishing Corses not only upon the points of the Compasse, but upon every degree of the Horizon, and giveth the distance of any Travers for the particular elevation of minuts, yea, & lesse parts assure your selfe: it giveth longitudes and latitudes to the minute second and third: in so great certaintie, as that by no other meanes the like can be performed: it teacheth the nature of Angles and Triangles, as well Sphericall as plaine superficiall and solide Commensurations, the effect of lynes straght, circular, and paradoxall, the quantities and proportions of parallells, the nature of Horizons, with every particular distinction of any alteration whatsoever, that may in Navigation be required to a most wonderfull precise certaintie: for there can nothing be required, that by this heavenly harmony of numbers shall not be most copiously manifested to the Seamans admiration and great content: the orderly practise whereof to the best of my poore capacitie I purpose to make knowne, if I may perceive my paines already taken, to be received in good part which I distrust not but all honest minded Seamen, and Pylots of reputation will gratefully embrace, onely in regard of my friendly good will towardes them, for it is not in respect of my paines, but of my love, that I would receive favourable curtesie.

How may the Poles height be knowne by the Globe?

There are divers wayes to finde the Poles height by the Globe, as well from the Meridian as upon the same, but sith before I have sufficiently taught how by the Sunnes Meridian altitude, the Poles height may be found, I will therefore in this place speake no further thereof, but for the other kindes it may be knowne as followeth.

How by the Sunnes rising or setting, the Poles height may be knowne.

By your Compasse of variation or some magneticall instrument, observe at the Sunne rising, upon what degree of the Horizon the center toucheth according to the true horizontall position

position of the Magnet, all variation duely considered, that being knowne, search in the Tables of the Ephimerides, for the Suns place in the Ecliptick, at the time of your obseruation, then bring that place or degree of the Ecliptick wherein you find the Sunne to be to the Horizon, and mooue the Meridian of the Globe as occasion requireth, vntill that obserued degree of the Horizon & the Sunnes place in the Eclipticke doe iustly touch together, for then is the Pole in his due Eleuation, as by the intersection of the Horizon and Meridian may appeare, in like sort you may find the Poles altitude, by any knowne fixed Starre in the Horizon.

To finde the Poles height by the Sunne, vpon any point of the Compasse.

By the Compasse of variation, rectified to the true Horizontall position, obserue the Sunne vntill he come to any poynt thereof at your pleasure, and in the same instant take the Suns height from the Horizon, then bring the Quarta altitudo to that poynt of the Compasse vpon the Horizon of the Globe where you obserue the Sunne to be, there holding the Quarta altitudo steadie, mooue the Globe vntill you bring the degree of the Eclipticke (wherein the Sunne is at the time of your obseruation) vnto the edge of the Quarta altitudo, if it fall vpon that degree of altitude as was the Sunnes obserued height, then doth the Pole stand to his true Eleuation, but if it agree not, you must eleuate or depresse the Pole as occasion requireth, rectifying the Zenith answerable thereunto. And againe make tryall as at the first bringing the place of the Sunne to the Quarta altitudo, and setting the same vpon the obserued poynt of the Compasse, vntill it agree in all respects with your obseruation, and then the Meridian sheweth in his intersection with the Horizon, the eleuation of the Pole from the Horizon.

To finde the Poles height by any giuen Azumuth by the Sunne being aboue the Horizon.

By your Magneticall instrument, or Compasse of variation, obserue the Azumuth of the Sunne at any time in the fore-noone,

noone, or afternoone, the neerer the Sunne is to the Horizon, the better shall be your obseruation, and at the same instant take the height of the Sunne from the Horizon, keepe these two numbers in memory, and note that the Azumuth be obserued according to the true position of the Horizon, by hauing good regard to the variation of the Compasse, then bring the Quarta altitudo to the place of the Sunne in the Eclipticke, and set that degree of the Sunnes place in the Eclipticke vpon the obserued degree of altitude by the graduation of the Quarta altitudo, and if the end thereof at the same instant do fall right vpon the obserued degree of Azumuth, then is the Pole in his due Eleuation: if not, then rayse or lay the Pole as occasion requireth, alwayes regarding that you place the Zenith answerable to the Poles altitude, and then againe bring the Sunnes place to his altitude vpon the Quarta altitudo, and looke againe whether the end thereof doe touch the obserued degree of Azumuth vpon the Horizon, if not, you must prosecute this order, vntill at one instant the place of the Sunne be vpon his true almicanter, by the edge of the Quarta altitudo, and that the end of the Quarta altitudo doe also touch the obserued degree of Azumuth vpon the Horizon, for then is the Pole in his true eleuation, as by the Meridian and the Horizon will appeare.

To find the Poles height by the Sunne by any two giuen Azumuths and altitudes, not regarding the true horizontall position or needles variations.

Because there may great errors be commited in the former obseruations, vnlesse the Compasse be perfectly well rectified, so as it may respect the true parts or distinctions of the Horizon, it is not amisse to enforme you how without regard of variation, the Poles height may be found.

Therefore by your Magneticall instrument or Compasse of variation, obserue the Sunnes Azumuth, without regard of the true Horizontall position, and at the same instant obserue also his altitude from the Horizon, keepe those two numbers in memory, then after the Sunne hath mooued a poynt or two poynts of the Compasse more or lesse at your discretion, obserue againe his

his Azumuth and altitude as at the first, then consider the arke of the Horizon, through which the Sunne hath mooued betweene these two obseruations, for by the two obseruations of the Suns altitude, and by the degrees of Azumuth through which the Sun hath moued, the Poles height is thus knowne: First, set the Globe to the eleuation of the place wherein you are as neere as you can gesse, and bring the Zenith to the like latitude from the Equator, as the poles eleuation is from the Horizon, then bring the Quarta altitudo to the place of the Sunne vpon the Ecliptick, for the time of your obseruation, there place the Sun vpon the first obserued altitude by the degrees of the Quarta altitudo, and not the degree of the Horizon which the Quarta altitudo then toucheth: this done, bring the Sunnes place to the second obserued altitude, by mooning the Quarta altitudo and the Globe vntill the degree of the Suns place in the Eclipticke, and the degree of his altitude vpon the Quarta altitudo doe meete. Then againe consider the degrees of the Horizon, which the end of the Quarta altitudo toucheth, and note the arke of the Horizon contained betweene your two obseruations, of how many degrees it consisteth, if it agree with the obseruations made by your Magneticall instrument, then doth the Pole stand in his true altitude, if not, you must either raise or depresse the Pole, and againe prosecute the former practise, vntill you find such Azumuths and altitudes vpon the Globe, as you found by your Magneticall obseruations, for then the Pole doth stand in his true altitude, and then doth also appeare the true Azumuth of both your obseruations, which if it agree not with your Compasse, then is your Compasse varied, and may hereby be corrected, so that this doth not onely giue the poles height, but also the true Horizontall position without errour.

To finde the poles height by taking the Sunnes altitude aboue the Horizon, so that the precise time of any such obseruation be knowne.

If you desire at any time of the day to know the Poles height, as at 8. 9. or 10. of the clocke, &c. marke diligently the time of your obseruation, at what instant you doe obserue the Sunnes altitude

altitude from the Horizon, the time and altitude thus knowne, bring the place of the Ecliptick wherein the Sunne is at the time of youre obseruation directly vnder the Meridian, there holding the Globe steadie, bring the Index of the Circulus horarius to the houres of 12 or noone, then moue the Globe vntill the Index come to the houre of your obseruation, there hold the Globe steadie, then bring the Quarta altitudo to the place of the Sunne in the Ecliptick, if it agree with your obserued altitude, then doth the Pole stand in his true eleuation, if not, moue the Meridian by raising or depressing the Pole as occasion requireth, vntill you bring the altitude and the houre to agree, and then you haue the poles height, and by the end of the Quarta altitudo doth also appeare the degrée of Azimuth, whereupon the Sunne was at the time of your obseruation, and note that in raising or depressing the pole of the Globe, you must also place the Zenith so far from the Equinoctiall, as the Pole is from the Horizon, for this is a generall rule, that so much as the Pole is eleuated from the Horizon, so much is the latitude of the Zenith from the Equator, therefore you must allwayes bring the Zenith and altitude to agrée, whensoeuer you alter the eleuation, be it neuer so little.

To finde the Poles height by any two obseruations of the Sunnes altitude, not regarding the houre of the day, or any horizontall position of the Magnet, so that you know the distance of time betweene the said obseruations.

Although there be some difficultie in giuing the true time of any obseruations at the Sea, by reason of the alterations of Horizons, and of the needles variation, yet it is a matter most easie by a góod houre glasse, halfe houre glasse, and minute glasse, to measure the distance of time betwéene any two obserued altitudes, you may therefore vpon that ground find the poles height with great facilitie at any time, by the Sunne or any fixed Star, in this sort.

Consider in what place of the Ecliptick the Sunne is at any time of your obseruation, bring that place to the Meridian, there with a blacke lead by móouing the Globe describe a parallell to the Equator, answerable to the Sunnes diurnall motion and decliclination for the same instant, then if betweene your obseruations there be an houre, two houres more or lesse at your pleasure, as by your running glasses may be knowne, you must allow for euery houre 15. deg. of the Equator, for so much ascendeth euery houre, and for euery foure minutes one degree, and for euery minute $\frac{1}{4}$ of a degree, then knowing by this order how many degrees the Sunne is mooued betweene your two obseruations, you must vpon the parallell which you draw make two notes, so many degrees asunder as the Sunne hath mooued between your obseruations, which may be done in this sort: bring the place wherein the Sunne is vnder the Meridian, and marke what degree of the Equator is then vnder the Meridian, the Globe so standing vpon your parallell close by the Meridian, make the first note or marke, then turne the Globe, and reckon the degrees of the Equator that passe vnder the Meridian, vntill so many be past as was your obseruation, there againe holde the Globe steadie, and vpon your parallell close by the Meridian make your second note or marke, then knowing the Sunnes altitude at both the obseruations, you must bring the Quarta altitudo to the first note made vpon your parallell, there holding the Globe steadie, the Quarta altitudo, and marke agreeing in altitude, bring the Quarta altitudo to the second note, if that doe also agree with your former obserued altitude, then both the Globe stand in his true Eleuation, if not, you must eleuate or depresse the Pole by discretion, vntill you bring the two obserued altitudes of the Sunne to agree with the two markes which you made vpon your described parallell, and then is the Pole at his true eleuation: and what is spoken of the Sunne, the like may be done by any knowne fixed Starre. I hold this conclusion to be very necessary, pleasant, and easie for the Seamans purpose.

To find the true place of the Sunne in the Ecliptick at all times

Because it is most necessarily required in the former practises, that the Sunnes true place in the Ecliptick be at all times knowne, I thinke it not amisse to enforme you how the same may be done.

The

The chiefest and most certaine meane to know the same, is by the tables of the Ephemerides, but those tables wanting, the Seaman may in this sort doe it: by the Regiment seeke out the declination of the Sunne, that being knowne, bring the Zenith vpon the Meridian, so many degrees & minutes from the Equator as is the Sunnes declination, then moove the Globe vntill some degree of the Ecliptické doe come directly vnder the poynt of the Zenith, for that is the Sunnes place: you must further consider, whether it be betweene March and June, for then you must finde the degree in that quarter of the Ecliptick, contained betweene ♈ and ♋: if it be betweene June and September, you must finde the degree in that quarter of the Ecliptick, contained betweene ♋, and ♎, &c. of the rest.

It may allso be knowne vpon the Horizon of the Globe by a Calender Circle that is there described, in this sort: first search the day of your moneth wherein you desire to know the Sunnes declination, and directly against the same degree which standeth for that day, doth allso stand the degree of the Zodiac wherein the Sunne is at the same time, in a circle representing the Zodiac, and described vpon the Horizon.

But if it be Leape yeare, you must not take the precise day of the moneth wherein you see the Sunnes place, but the next day following and against that day seeke the declination.

To finde the Poles height by any two knowne fixed Starres.

WHen you see any two fixed Starres, which you know to be both at one instant in the horizon, vpon your Globe search for those Starres, and bring one of them to touch the Horizon of the Globe, if the other doe not likwise touch the Horizon, you must raise or depresse the Pole by discreete mooving of the Meridian, vntill you bring both those Starres to be at one instant in the Horizon, for then the Globe doth stand to his true elevation.

To finde the Poles height by any two knowne fixed Starres another way.

WHen you see any fixed Starre that you know to be in the Horizon, you must presently take the height of some other Starre, that you likewise know, before the first be risen from the Horizon, then vpon your Globe search for the Starre that you obserued in the Horizon, bring that Starre to the Horizon of the Globe, there holding the Globe steadie, bring the Quarta altitudo to the other Starre whose altitude you obserued, if it agree vpon the Quarta altitudo with the obserued altitude, then the Globe doth stand to his true eleuation, if not, you must by discretion raise or lay the Pole, vntill you find the one Starre in the Horizon, and the other vpon his true obserued altitude, for then the Pole doth stand to his true eleuation.

To finde the Poles height at any time by any two knowne fixed Starres.

WIth your crosse staffe take the distance of any two stars from your Zenith, which must be done with as much expedition as may be, their distances so knowne, with a paire of Compasses, measure so many degrees vpon the Equator, as is the distance of the first obserued Starre, with another paire of Compasses doe the like for the second obserued Starre, vpon the first Star set one point of the Compasses that tooke his distance, and vpon the second Star set likewise one foote of the Compasses that tooke his distance, bring the other two feete of the Compasses to meete together, there make a marke, for that is the parallell wherein you be, that marke is the Zenith, bring it to the Meridian by mooving the Globe, and there will appeare the latitude desired, for so many degrees and minutes as that marke is from the Equator, so much is the Pole eleuated aboue the Horizon. This conclusion the Seaman ought to haue in good esteeme.

To know the precise houre at all times by the Sunne

FOr the finding of the houre of the day by the Globe, it is necessary that the Poles height be first knowne, therefore set the Pole to his true eleuation, and the Zenith to his answerable latitude, then bring the place of the Sunne in the Ecliptick vnder the Meridian, there holding the Globe steadie, place the Index of the Circulus horarius vpon 12, of the clocke or noone your Globe thus

thus ordered, then with your Crosse staffe take the Suns height from the Horizon, that being knowne you must bring the place of the Sunne to the Quarta altitudo, by mooving the Globe and Quarta altitudo untill the place of the Sunne doe agree with the observed altitude, there holding the Globe that he mooue not, the Index doth shew upon the Circulus horarius, the true houre desired.

To finde the houre of the night by any knowne fixed Starre.

SEt the Globe to his true altitude, and the Zenith to his answerable latitude, you must also place the Index of the Circulus horarius upon the houre of 12. or noone, by bringing the Sunnes place under the Meridian, &c. as before you did by the Sunne, then take the height of any knowne fixed Starre, bring that Starre to the Quarta altitudo, by moouing the Globe and Quarta altitudo, untill the Starre come to his true obserued altitude, there holding the Globe steadie, the Index doth shew upon the Circulus horarius, the true time of your obseruation.

To know the length of the dayes and nights, at all times, and in all places.

THe place and time being giuen wherein you desire to know the length of the day or night, first set the Globe to his altitude for the place, then search the place of the Sunne in the Ecliptick, for the time wherein you seeke the dayes length, bring that place of the Sunne under the Meridian, there holding the Globe that he moue not, place the Index of the Circulus horarius upon the houre 12. or noone, then turne the Globe untill you bring the place of the Sunne to touch the East part of the horizon, there holding the Globe, you shall see by the Index of the Circulus horarius, the true time of the Sunnes rising, then bring the place of the Sunne to the West part of the Horizon, & you shall there see the true time of the Sunnes setting, whereby the length of the day and night doth most plainly appeare. And this may suffice for the use of the Globe, necessary for the Sea-mans use.

I might here recite the triple rising and setting of the Starres, Cosmice, Acronice, and Heliace, the ascentions right & oblique, the dawning and twy light, houres equall and unequall, ordinary and planetary, dayes naturall and artificiall, the triple rising of of the Sunne, Equinoctiall and Solsticiall, Circles of position, with their use and nature, the horoscope and domifying distinctions of the heauens, the planets, their motions, retrogradiations, and excentricitie of their orbs, horologie, and many other most pleasant conclusions: but because they doo in no sort appertaine to the Seamans use, I therefore omit them, as matters more troublesome then profitable for him, expecting from some learned Mathematician a worke of worthy esteeme, wherein these and many other excellent conclusions shall by cunning demonstration be made knowne unto us.

Of the Crosse staffe and his demonstration.

The Crosse staffe is an artificiall quadrant, geometrically proiected into that forme as an instrument of greatest ease and exactest use in Nauigation, by which in any naturall disturbance of weather (the Sunne or Starres appearing) the Poles height may be knowne, when the Astrolabie or quadrant are not to be used. Conueying the use of the quadrant from the beame of the Sunne to the beames of the eye, for whereas by the quadrant the Sunne beame perceiuing the Dioptra sheweth his height, so by the Crosse staffe the beame of the eye conueyed to the Sun or Starre, doth likewise giue their height. The demonstration whereof is thus.

Make a plaine square consisting of foure right angles, as is the square, I. o. h. n. the angle I. shall be assigned the Center of the quadrant where placing one foote of your Compasses, stretch the other foote to the angle n. and therewith describe a quarter of a circle, as is the arke o. d. n. then from the center I. to his opposit angle h. draw a right line, by which line the quadrant o. d. n. is diuided into two equall parts, in the point d. diuide the arke d. n. into 90 equall parts, drawing from the center I. lines through euery of those diuisions touching in the line n. h. as by this figure appeareth: then consider the length of your transuersary, & take halfe thereof, laying it upon the line I. o. in the point S. from that point S. draw a parallell to the line I. n. as is the line S. y. and as that line doth intersect the diuision of the halfe quadrant, so shall be the degrees of the Crosse staffe, and note that the sides of the square, must be as long as the staffe that is graduated.

Because

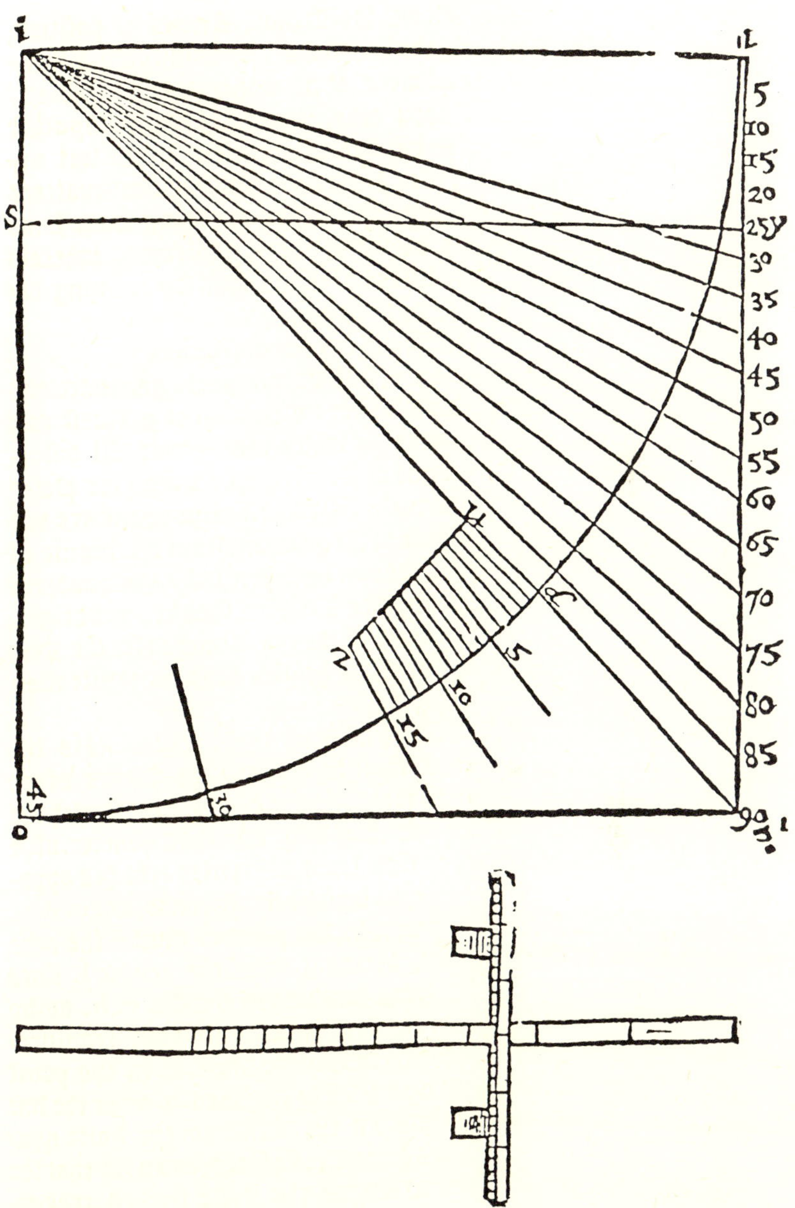

Because the staffe should be of unreasonable length to containe

 more

more then 60. degrees, therefore to keepe him in due forme for the ease of his vse, and that the complement of 90. degrees should be contained vpon the staffe, the other 30. are artificially proiected vpon the transuersary, as by this demonstration appeareth, and in this sort consider the length of your staffe from that point S. to the last intersection which endeth in 30. degrees, lay downe the length of the line I. h. at the point of v. from that point draw a right line, cutting the line I. h. to right angles as is the line v. a. being iust the length of halfe the transuersary: then diuide the arke o, d. into 45. equall parts, accompting from the point d. to the point o. then from the angle I. draw right lines to the first 15. of those parts, and as those lines doe cut the line v. a. so must the transuersary be graduated on both his parts, whereunto vanes being framed, your staffe is finished to your vse.

There is a staffe of another proiection, which I find by practise to be an instrument of very great ease, and certaintie at the Sea, the Sunne not being more then 45. degrees aboue the Horizon, whose vse is contrary to the other before demonstrated, for by this staffe the beame of the Sunne shadowing vpon the transuersary, doth thereby giue the height most precisely, not regarding how to place the center of the staffe to the eye, for the correction of the parallax of the sight, and without looking vpon the Sunne, whose demonstration is thus

Draw two right lines, cutting each other at right angles, as doe the lines d. v. and d. s. vpon the angle d. describe a quarter circle, as is the arke v. s. diuide that quadrant into two equall parts by the line d. n. cutting the quadrant into the point h. diuide the arke s. h. into 45. equall parts or degrees, drawing lines from the center d. to euery of those diuisions, then from the point I. bring the third part of the line d. s. vpon the center d. describe an arke of a circle, as is the arke I, o. which is for the transuersary of this staffe, and the line d. s. is for the staffe, then from the point o. where the vpper end of the transuersary toucheth the line d. n. draw a parallell to the line d. s. as is the line o. y. and as that line doth cut the lines drawn from the center d. so must the staffe d. s. be graduated, laying it vpon the line o. y. putting that part of the staffe where the point I. toucheth, vpon the point o. and then from the point I. lay downe the degrees, as are the intersections vpon the line o. y. and so is the staffe graduated.

The

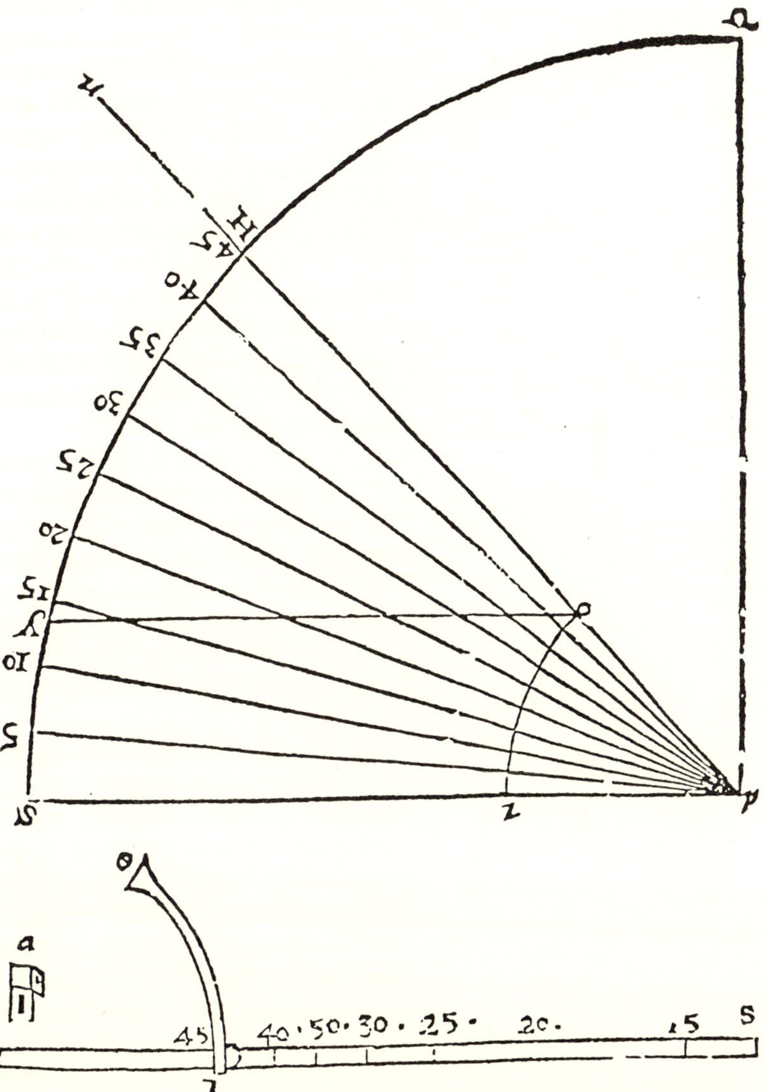

The transuersary at the point i must haue an artificial hole made for the staffe to run in, as other staues haue, also there must be a plate of brasse with a soccat to be set to the center of the staffe, as is the figure a. in the midst whereof there must be a slitte, through which the sight must be conueyed to the Horizon, and this plate must receiue the shadow of the transuersary, and so the staffe is finished.

How

How is the vse of this staffe?

The vse of this staffe is altogether contrary to the other, for the center of this staffe where the brasse plate is fastned, must be turned to that part of the Horizon which is from the Sunne, & with your backe toward the Sunne, by the lower edge of the halfe crosse: & through the slitte of the plate you must direct your sight onely to the Horizon, & then mouing the transuersary as occasion requireth, vntill the shadow of your vpper edge of the transuersary doe fall directly vpon the same slitte or long hole, and also at the same instant you see the horizon through the slitte, and then the transuersary sheweth the height desired.

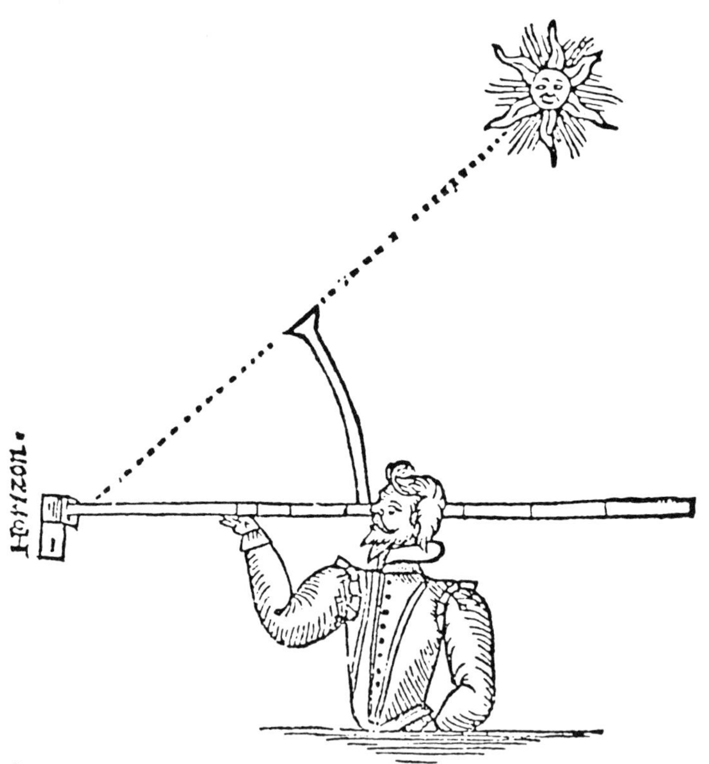

Finding by practise the excellency of the Crosse staffe aboue all other instruments, to satisfie the Seamans expectation, and also knowing that those instruments whose degrées are of largest capacitie, are instruments of most certainty. I haue very carefully laboured to search a good and demonstrable meane how a Crosse staffe might be protected, not only to containe

taine large degrées, but also to auoyd the vncertaintie of ẏ sight, by disorderly placing of the staffe to the eye, which demonstration I haue found, & haue had the instrument in practise, aswell vnder the Sun, as in other climates, but because it hath a large demõstratiõ, with manifold vses, I here omit to manifest ẏ same, purposing to write a particular treatise thereof, notwithstãding his forme & vse, by picture I haue thought good to expresse.

This staffe is a yard long, hauing 2. halfe crosses, the one circular, the other straight, the longest not 14 inches, yet this staffe doth contain ẏ whole 90. degrées, the shortest degrée being an inch & ¼ long, wherein the minuts are particularly & very sensibly laid down, by which staffe not regarding the parallax of your sight, nor looking vpon ẏ Sunne, but onely vpon the horizon, the Suns height is most precisely knowne, as well and as easily in the Zenith, as in any other part of the heauen. Then which instrument (in my opinion) the Seaman shall not finde any so good, & in all Climates of so great certainty, the inuention & demonstration whereof I may boldly chalenge to appertaine vnto my selfe (as a portiõ of the talent which God hath bestowed vpõ me) I hope without abuse or offence to any.

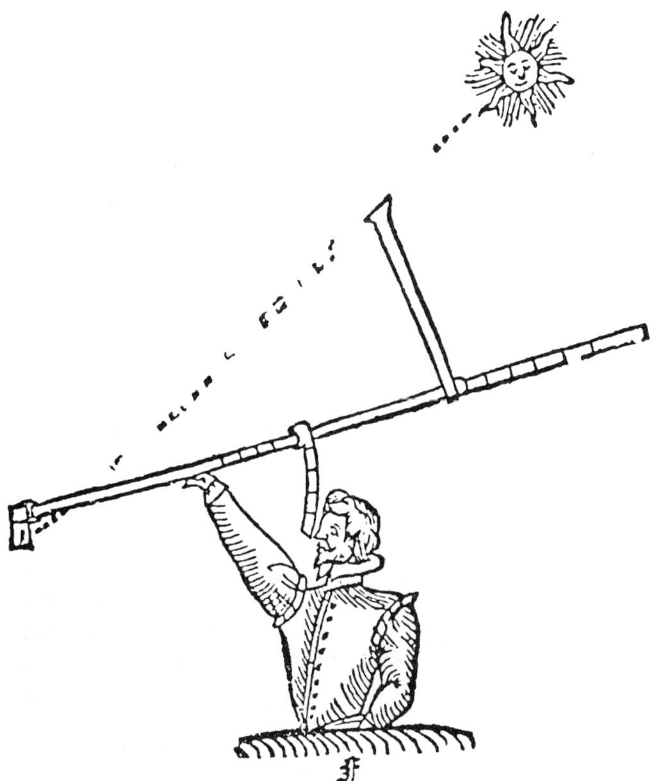

Of the Quadrant

A Quadrant is the fourth part of a circle, containing 90. degrees, and repreſenteth the diſtance betweene the Horizon and Zenith, being an excellent inſtrument vpon the ſhore, to performe any Aſtronomicall obſeruations, but for a Seaman it is to no purpoſe: and although there may be very much written of the commodious and excellent vſes of the Quadrant, yet not being an apt inſtrument for Sea obſeruations, it ſhall be from my purpoſe to write further thereof, and therefore the onely laying downe of his forme may at this preſent ſuffice

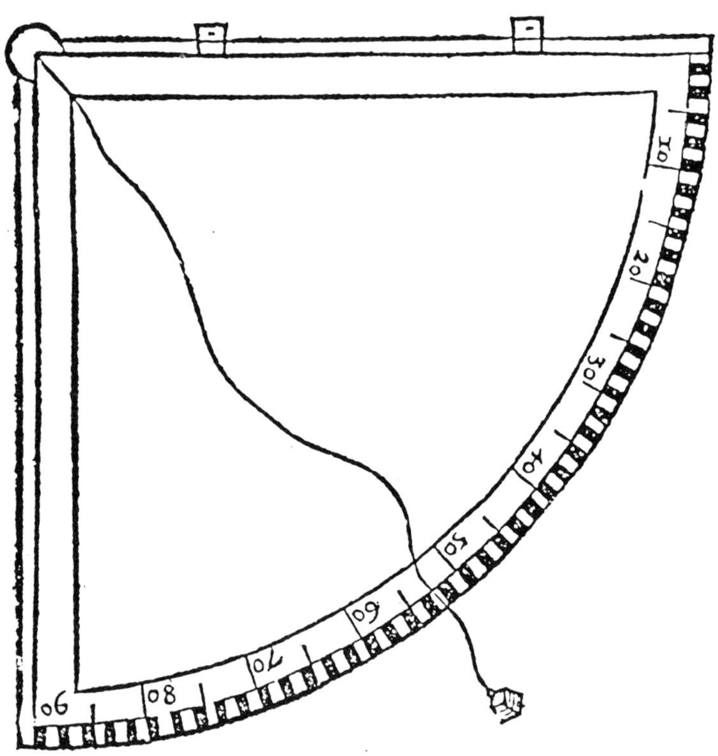

Of the Aſtrolabie.

AN Aſtrolabie is the repreſentation of a great circle, containing four Quadrants or 360. degrees, which inſtrument hath bin in long vſe among Seamen, and it is an excellent inſtrument, being rightly vnderſtood and ordered, but ſith the vulgar Aſtrolabie with his vſe to euery

Seaman

Seaman sufficiently knowne, it should be vaine labour for me to lay downe his vse and demonstration: therefore by his forme it shall suffice to expresse him.

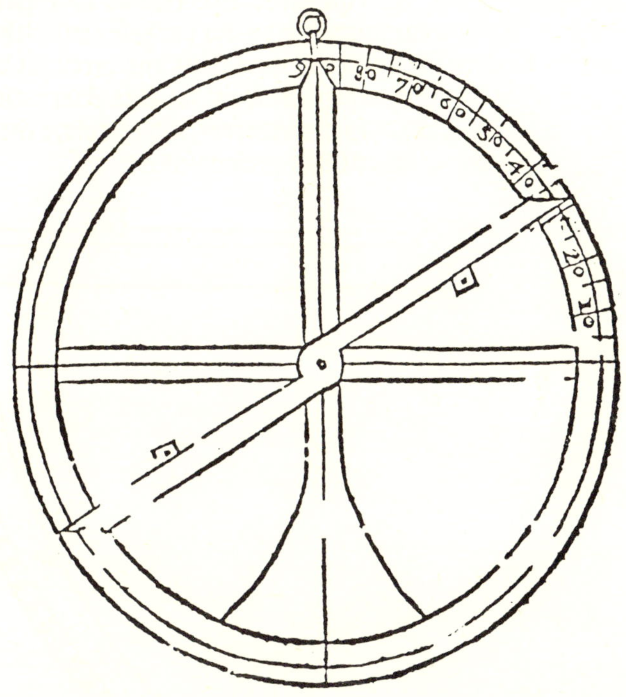

There hath beene great paines taken by many, for the enlarging of the degrees contained in an Astrolabie, among which there is a proiection to conuey the degrees of a Quadrant into the concauitie of an Astrolabie, whereby those degrees shall be double, to any other Astrolabie, of the same quantitie, so that the Sunbeame pearcing a hole made in the side of the Astrolabie, is thereby carried to the degrees noted, in the opposite concaue part, as by his forme may appeare

Also my selfe labouring in the same matter, haue found a meane whereby an Arke of a Quadrant whose side is 10. foote, may be conueyed into an Astrolabie of 10. inches diameter, whose dioptra shall cut his lymbe to right angles, and shall performe the comple-

ment

ment of 90. degrees, as amply and as effectually as by the Quadrant it may in any sort be done.

Whose demonstration, together with the demonstration of my staffe, I purpose God willing, at large to manifest: But there can be no inuention that can establish the certainty of the vse of either Quadrant or Astrolabie at the Sea, for vnlesse it be in very smooth water, there can be no certaintie of any obseruation by those instruments, whereby the Seaman may rest assured of the altitude which he seeketh, but the obseruations made by the Crosse staffe, are without all distrust of errour, and therefore no instrument may compare with the excellencie of this Crosse staffe for the Seasnam vse

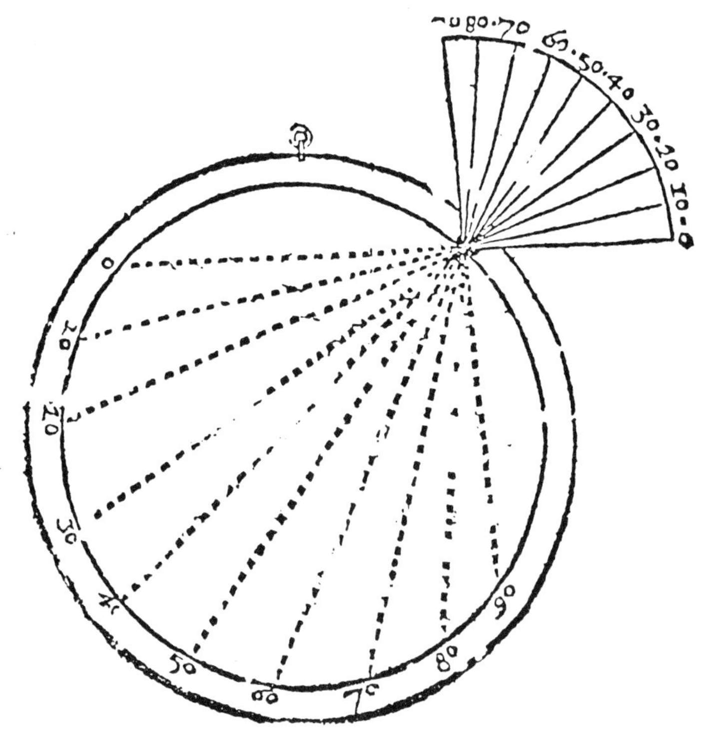

FINIS.

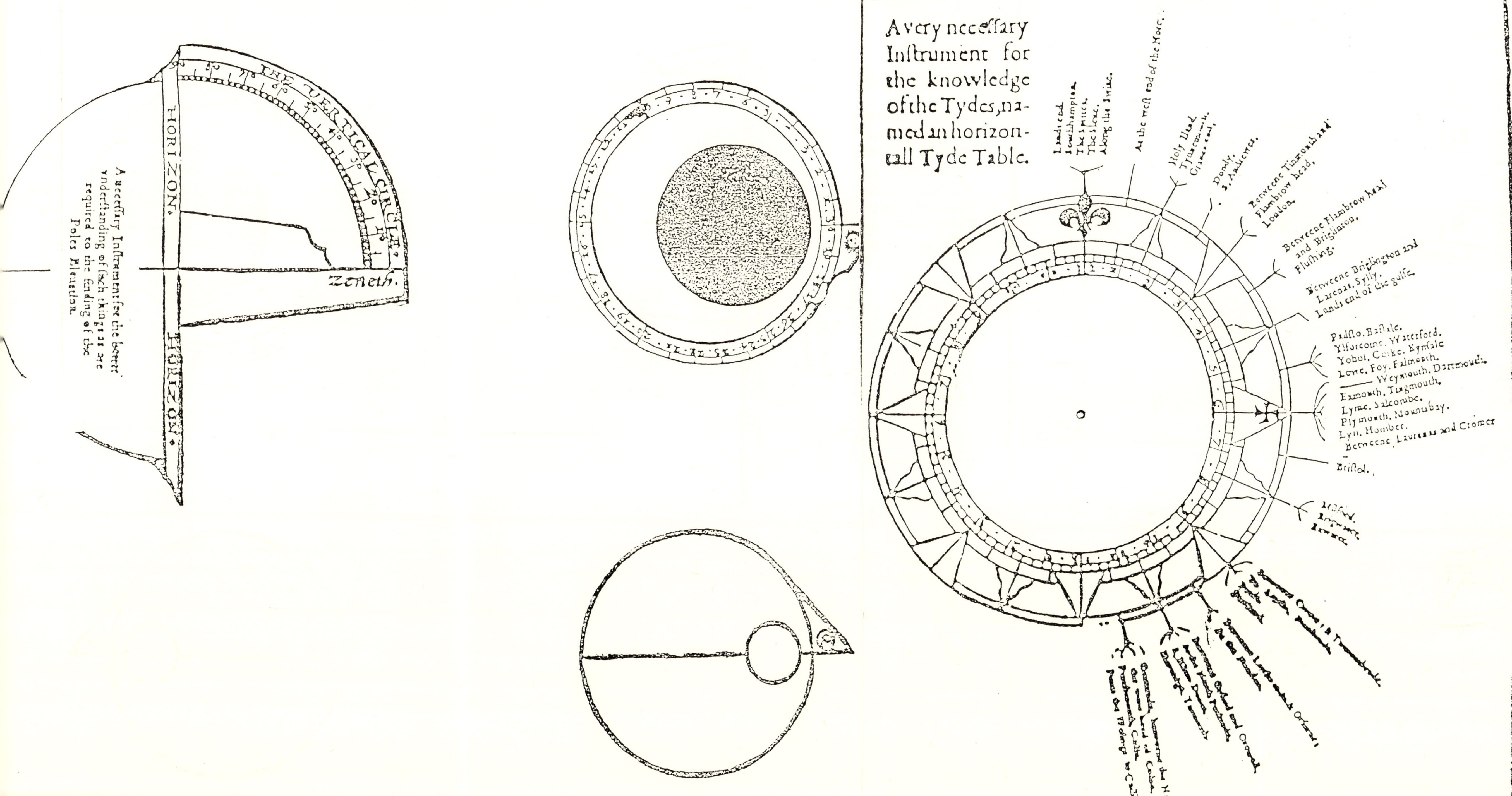
A very necessary Instrument for the knowledge of the Tydes, named an horizontall Tyde Table.
THE VERTICALL CIRCLE
HORIZON
HORIZON
Zeneth.
A necessary Instrument for the better understanding of such things as are required to the finding of the Poles Elevation.
Bristol.